AUTUMN LEAVES

A DNA MEMOIR

SHARON BETH

CONTENTS

FOREWORD	vii
PROLOGUE	1
CHAPTER ONE: LIVIN' IN RESEDA	5
CHAPTER TWO: DNA	15
CHAPTER THREE: INTERFAITH LOVE	20
CHAPTER FOUR: THE SIMPLEST ANSWER	29
CHAPTER FIVE: JACK	33
CHAPTER SIX: SHEILA	45
CHAPTER SEVEN: DANA	56
CHAPTER EIGHT: JUDY	63
CHAPTER NINE: QUESTIONS	69
CHAPTER TEN: JEAN	78
CHAPTER ELEVEN: RESULTS	90
CHAPTER TWELVE: COUSINS	92
CHAPTER THIRTEEN: BURLESQUE	95
CHAPTER FOURTEEN: MARYANN	104
CHAPTER FIFTEEN: DISCOVERY	107
CHAPTER SIXTEEN: FLORIDA	116
CHAPTER SEVENTEEN: AUTUMN LEAVES	127
CHAPTER EIGHTEEN: DNA ANGEL	131
CHAPTER NINETEEN: MOM	136
EPILOGUE	143
FINAL THOUGHTS	149
ACKNOWLEGEMENTS	151
ABOUT THE AUTHOR	155
RESOURCES	157

Autumn Leaves: A DNA Memoir Copyright © 2025 by Sharon Beth. All rights reserved. No part of this publication may be reproduced, distributed, or transmitted in any form or by any means, including photocopying, recording, or other electronic or mechanical methods, without the prior written permission of the author and publisher, except in the case of brief quotations embodied in critical reviews and certain other noncommercial uses permitted by copyright law.

Printed in the United States of America

ISBN 979-8-9996603-5-0 hardback

ISBN 979-8-9996603-9-8 paperback

ISBN 979-8-9996603-0-5 E-book Kindle

Library of Congress Control Number: 2025916338

Book design and cover revisions by Aliena Cameron

Initial cover design by Roberta Morris

First Edition

Maybe one day I'll fly next to you . . .

FOREWORD

As a child, I remember being told many so-called truths: I shouldn't read in the dark or sit too close to the television screen because "it would hurt my eyes." I was also told that "people can't have babies until they're married," which made me believe that conception actually occurred at the altar! Additionally, I heard, "You can't play in the rain; you'll catch pneumonia!"

As a child, I accepted all those little white lies from my family as truths without questioning them. While I now understand that these statements were meant to keep me in line, I never expected that anyone might lie about more significant matters, such as our family background.

As far as I was concerned, everything I'd been told about my family over the years *was* the truth, and there was never a reason to doubt my relatives.

As it turned out, I'd been completely misled for years . . . and when one truth shatters, it leads you to question everything else, which is how this book began—after a revelation that left me with more questions than answers. So I did what I'd always done when I needed to process or figure something out. I started writing.

FOREWORD

The act of putting a pen, or paintbrush, to paper has always been an outlet for me—whether this be journaling, writing poems, drawing, or oil painting, which I took up in college. I naturally turned to one of these during points of tension in my life, like after a family death or a conflict with a close friend. For me, writing is a therapeutic tool, though I never set out to become a writer. Little did I know that one day I'd write a book! But after all that's happened, I felt compelled to do this. Even if you don't resonate with every aspect of the story you're about to read, or if your story is different, I'd like to think this book can offer hope to those who have also experienced a shattering of truth in some way. Maybe someone you love has been lying to you. Or you recently learned you were adopted. Or you have a sibling(s) you never knew about. Betrayal cuts deep, and whatever your story is, it matters and there's hope.

In addition to writing about what happened, I want to honor my family's heritage and legacy throughout this story. I believe it is important to preserve both the joyful moments and the struggles—the mistakes and heartaches, but also the resilience. This narrative explores all of that while also addressing a truth that was taken away for sixty-three years. My hope is for you to know you're not alone in whatever challenges you are currently facing, and that through my story, you'll find some comfort.

The stories, locations, and events recounted in this book are true to the best of my knowledge and supported by family interviews, newspaper archives, book citations and DNA evidence. Although multiple perspectives exist, this narrative is told entirely from my viewpoint. Some names have been altered or left out for privacy. While scenes and dialogues are true, they may have been slightly modified for clarity.

PROLOGUE

DECEMBER 2024

The bright light of the reel flashed on the screen for a moment, and then the darker shapes gradually came into focus, revealing the woman I'd admired so much as a child. It was my dear Grandma Sheila. The vibrant 8mm film reel captures her and my mother, who looks around one year old, in 1955, enjoying a day at the beach.

It was late December 2024, and I was nearing the end of writing this book. But something had drawn me to watch this reel again. A sense, maybe, that it might contain answers I still hadn't found.

The film begins with Grandma Sheila standing in front of an off-white building waving at the camera while my mom is sitting in a stroller. There's nothing else around them apart from the end of a chain-link fence to their left. My mother has on short white dungarees, and there's a large white bow-styled barrette in her hair, clipped on the left side of her head. Grandma Sheila is wearing a backless one-piece swimsuit with a red-and-white checkered pattern. It has a delicate ruffle along the top and is secured by a halter-neck spaghetti-strap top. Her hair is dark and pinned up off her shoulders, exposing her ears and neck.

Grandma Sheila keeps waving as she lifts my mom from the stroller, grabbing her arm to make a waving gesture at the camera. She's mouthing words, but I can't make out what she's saying. If only the clip had sound! Then she starts walking toward the beach, my mom in her arms, past the chain-link fence. She has to take a fairly large step down to get to the sand. As she makes her way closer to the water, still carrying my mother, she turns around and waves repeatedly.

Grandma Sheila is very charismatic and cheerful on camera, constantly smiling, posing like a model, and waving. The video then cuts to a close-up of her and my mom, and a large portion of the backside of a building, different from the one at the start of the clip, with greenery surrounding it, appears. I felt certain I'd seen this place before, and not just from the last time I'd watched the reel, nearly twenty-two years ago. The sense of recognition was stronger than that. I couldn't put my finger on why it seemed so familiar, but many years later I'd figure out that the scenery matched old photographs I had.

I felt Grandma Sheila's immense love for my mom in this video as she hugs her tightly. As I watched, I thought how much I missed her warm smile, which I remember so well from when I was a child.

Grandma Sheila is now standing ankle-deep in the water, bending down and allowing my mom's toes to touch the surface. She keeps looking up and smiling at the camera and then goes a little deeper, bending at the waist as she holds my mom, belly down, skimming the surface of the water, slowly moving her back and forth. My back hurt just watching her bend like that. Later, the video cuts to Grandma Sheila lying on the sand on her left side with her back turned away from the camera. My mom is sitting up, resting against her stomach. For a brief moment, she looks toward the water with her hand up to her mouth and no expression on her face. I wondered what she was thinking about at that moment. The camera stays on her and my mom until she turns and notices. She turns around, laughs, and motions to the person behind the camera, who'd snuck up on them, to stop filming. She makes another "quit that" gesture with her hand and then shades her eyes to look off into the distance toward the water again. She offers one final smile, and the film ends with Grandma Sheila changing my mom's clothing on the sand.

Back in 2002, I'd transferred all twenty-four 8mm film reels belonging to my grandparents onto a DVD, including this one. I don't know why on this day in late December 2024 I was drawn to this particular reel of my grandmother and my mom on the beach. I hadn't watched these films since we had a big family viewing over twenty-two years ago when my Grandpa Jack was still alive. But on this day, as soon as I finished watching, something kept nagging me about this reel. I wanted to figure out what it was, so I watched it again from the start—multiple times. I still couldn't shake the strong sense of recognition. Why were the images of my mom and grandmother on the beach in their bathing suits so familiar to me?

Fortunately, my parents kept all the originals after I converted the reels, so I called them that night and asked them to pull them out and send me photos of each one. Each reel was enclosed in an individual brown cardboard box that Grandma Sheila had labeled many years ago. She was careful and thorough, and the description on each label explicitly matched the video's content: "Children with poodle," "Vacation at Colonial Terrace #1," "Colonial Terrace bad light," "Children on swing," "Mayfair Club, Michelle on bike," "Mom and Pop and family," "Michelle's 6th birthday," "Michelle at camp," "Lake George," "Disneyland," "Boat ride to Indian village," and so on.

However, I couldn't find any boxes labeled with "Michelle and I," "Michelle on the beach," "Beach day," "Baby Michelle," or simply "Beach." I thought that was strange, given that twenty-three out of the twenty-four reels were labeled so accurately.

I kept carefully scanning each one to see if I'd somehow missed it. And then I noticed a lonely box among the others. It was completely blank.

I remembered seeing a blank box when I converted these twenty-two years ago, but I never thought anything about it back then. I called my dad and told him I had to see the reel inside the blank box, so he agreed to mail it to me. When the reel arrived a few days later, I opened it up and inserted it into my film converter, and there it was: my grandmother and my mother at the beach.

Why didn't Grandma Sheila label this particular reel? I wondered. *Did she forget? Did her pen run out of ink? Or . . . was she hiding something?*

Unlabeled reel from 1955

CHAPTER ONE: LIVIN' IN RESEDA

1978–2015

I was born in 1978 and grew up in the city of Reseda, a suburb in the Greater Los Angeles area of California. My immediate family includes my older sister, Rebecca, and my parents, Rob and Michelle, whom I'm very close to. I am married to an amazing man, Nathan, who's the same age as me, and we have four wonderful children all together. I met Nathan in 2003 along with his two children, who were two and six years old at the time, just before we turned twenty-five. Three years later, in 2006, we were married in Santa Barbara, California, and had our first child together at the age of thirty and our second at thirty-two. I absolutely love being a wife, mom, teacher, volunteer, believer, and now a grandma!

Growing up in the 1980s was awesome, as many of my fellow Gen Xers would agree. We LIVED. Before the internet became a part of our lives, my friends and I, who were considered "latchkey" kids, had parents who worked full-time. There was no such thing as helicopter parents hovering around, so we got to explore the neighborhood freely. We got lost, got hurt, and got rejected by other kids, but we took it all in stride. It helped us grow independent, tough, and emotionally resilient. If we wanted to play, we had to rely on our imaginations to entertain ourselves during bouts of boredom. If we wanted to eat, we made our own meals. If we wanted to see a friend, we had to get ourselves to their house. We were strong and resourceful, and I'm so grateful I grew up in that era.

I'm also reminded of my childhood whenever I hear Tom Petty's "Free Fallin'," where he sings about livin' in Reseda and dating a girl who loves her mama, Jesus, America, and horses. That was my childhood existence in a nutshell.

My next-door neighbor growing up was Anastasia (Ana). In 1984, my family had just moved into our first home, and she was my first friend on the block and my best friend for years. Ana and I had a close bond that made us inseparable, even though we had other special friends in the neighborhood and a three-and-a-half-year age difference. We were "buds." We climbed the cinder block wall that divided our yards and sat up there talking, writing notes to each other, and goofing around for hours until it was dark outside. Our wall crumbled in the 1994 Northridge earthquake, but we didn't care—we had easier access to each other after that! We made perfumes out of rose petals in the playhouse in my yard, climbed trees, and picked our neighbor's oranges and apricots when we were hungry. When we got bored of doing that, we played in the street all day, riding bikes, roller-skating around the block, and going on "adventures" with my sister and the other neighborhood kids. We drank from hoses, ate loads of junk food, and the only reason we didn't go outside was if we were grounded or sick. We LIVED.

On weekends I attended church, and from the ages of ten to fourteen I worked at a local pony-ride and petting zoo that Ana introduced me to. Sunrise to sundown was spent grooming, tacking, corralling, and riding horses. I was thrown off horses and stepped on more times than I can count. I was rammed in the legs by the most annoying goats and chased by the most aggressive geese. I constantly shoveled poop, lifted small children on and off the ponies, and got yelled at by the owner and the older kids who worked there because I was at the bottom of the pecking order.

While there are multiple perspectives, I remember the owner, Linda, was a loud, tough woman. She wasn't afraid of anyone, but almost everyone was afraid of her. There were expectations, and if you didn't meet them or you screwed up, she would scream and insult you with names like "Dingy" or "Airhead" in front of everyone, even in front of the customers. No matter how small or big your mistake was, she had little to no mercy for your feelings. And the older kids just followed her lead. Many days I would hide my tears, but I just kept working. You had to suck it up. You were there to work, and if you wanted to earn money, this was the job. If you didn't like it, there was the door. We drank warm Coca-Cola sodas and ate crunchy beef tacos from Taco Bell for lunch, which she sometimes provided for us.

Looking back on those long weekends, I can't help but feel lucky to have been part of Linda's farm. No matter how tough she was on us or how grueling and challenging I found the work environment, I wouldn't trade those days for anything. Linda's little farm was the only one in my immediate area that offered our community a place to work with ranch animals and learn horseback riding. I felt like I'd struck gold whenever she allowed me to ride for free in the big arena or the time she let me borrow a horse for a trail ride. I also felt like a hotshot when she handed me a whopping ten-dollar bill for an entire weekend of work. I appreciate all the life lessons I picked up while working on that farm, especially about taking care of animals and the value of hard work. It made everything worth it. As a bonus, I got to chat with Henry Winkler and Hulk Hogan, who used to visit the farm now and then. They always smiled and spoke gently toward me.

Many of the kids who worked on the farm owned a horse,

including Ana. One afternoon, I borrowed Ana's horse for a trail ride in Chatsworth Park and was thrown off. I knew better than to borrow her horse, who had a very bad habit of rearing up. But I wanted to go riding with friends, so I took my chances. I took a hit straight to the nose and was knocked unconscious and bloodied only to be found by joggers in the park who carried me to safety and helped me call my mom, who then took me to the hospital. After recovering, I decided I would never borrow Ana's or anyone's horse again. If I wanted to continue riding on the trails, I realized I had to make a change.

I had been saving up my money every weekend, and at the age of twelve, I was able to buy my own horse. I also had enough money to pay for the monthly boarding at White Oaks Stables in Chatsworth, where Ana also boarded her horse. My horse Stormy was a spunky six-year-old dapple-gray Arabian that stood about fourteen hands tall. Ana and I frequently enjoyed trail rides in Chatsworth Park together. By the end of the day, we were exhausted and filthy, but we were living our best lives. My Grandma Sheila, whom I was very close to, had just passed away, and having Stormy helped me cope during that difficult time.

When I quit working at the pony rides, the money ran out and I had to sell Stormy because the agreement with my parents was that she was *my* responsibility. I was nearly fifteen years old at that time, and I'd outgrown the working conditions on the farm. Letting go of Stormy was incredibly difficult. I tried to locate her years later but was unsuccessful. I can still see her sticking her sweet gray head out of the trailer and neighing as her new owner drove the trailer away. I went to church that morning in tears, and even as I write this today, it breaks my heart. I will always cherish her and can only hope she experienced a great life.

The same year I sold Stormy, Ana joined my youth group, and this added to our adventures together, especially at the camps, barbecues, and swim parties. I later ended up getting a new job on the weekends with *real* paychecks and friendlier bosses. But I'll never forget my first job on the farm. What Linda brought to our community was priceless, and those memories will always be a part of me. It was a great childhood, and Ana and I remain friends to this day.

In February 2011, when my son was eighteen months old, I took him for his first pony ride at Linda's farm. I felt like I was ten years old again, lifting him onto the pony and strapping him in. It was a special moment for me to share that with him (and my unborn daughter, whom I was pregnant with at the time). I was saddened that I didn't get to see Linda during that visit. She had passed away a few years before, and the farm officially shut down shortly after our visit. I drove past it later to see the empty lot of land, and a piece of me felt very empty, too.

As I approached my early twenties at the turn of the century, I became increasingly fascinated by my heritage. I've always deeply cherished my family, but perhaps I became more conscious of this following the challenges I experienced after high school, which made me appreciate my family in a way I'd taken for granted before. I was in a toxic relationship, and they supported me through those tough times. I don't know what I would have done without them. I recognized and appreciated how they were always there for me no matter what. I was reminded of how much I missed Grandma Sheila, who'd passed away when I was twelve, and how short and precious life was—and the fact that my remaining grandparents were getting older.

I realized that no one in my immediate family had kept a record of our heritage, and I felt it was crucial for someone to preserve our family's history to keep it alive. So in late 2000, I reached out to a distant maternal cousin named Bonnie, as she'd already done some research on my Grandpa Jack's family as well as her own family. I had a soft start with my maternal side, jotting down everything Bonnie shared.

Bonnie was a great resource for me. She taught me how to search for records and provided a lot of useful background information regarding my ancestors' names, birthplaces, migrations, and occupations. I became completely captivated as I slowly took on the role of keeper of my family's history. Later, I would be grateful for the careful notes and records I kept, even though at that time, I had no idea how much was missing from them or how misleading some of the information would be.

At the time I began my research, three of my four grandparents were still alive: Jack (my mother's dad), Rob (my father's dad), and Lorraine (my father's mom). Sheila (my mom's mother) had passed away. During my conversations with Grandpa Jack and Grandma Lorraine, I looked at multiple family pictures and they would describe each person and how he or she was related to me. They also told me little stories they remembered about family members.

Grandpa Rob lived over an hour away at the time and wasn't doing that well health-wise, so Grandma Lorraine filled in a lot. I heard stories from her about a cousin who played football for The Ohio State University and another cousin who lost a limb working in a factory. She also told me about her twin sister, Louise, and how they'd met and married a set of brothers: John and Rob. It was wild to me that two identical twin sisters married two brothers!

Grandma Lorraine married Grandpa Rob (whom my father is named after) and Louise married John. Sadly, the marriage didn't last between my grandparents—nor had Grandpa Rob's first marriage to a woman named Katherine, before Grandma Lorraine. Grandma Lorraine and Grandpa Rob divorced when my father was a teenager, but they both attended family events like the annual Christmas parties, which were held in a different family member's home each year. I have fond memories of being with them and seeing them interact like two friends. Grandma Lorraine lived a couple of miles away with my aunt in the home my father grew up in. She worked in the loan department for a bank for many years, smoked Virginia Slim cigarettes, drank her coffee black, and had a deep, distinguishable voice. It was easy to make her smile and laugh. She had the cutest giggle, and I never saw her upset. It was always a delight to visit her.

Grandpa Rob was a U.S. Army veteran who served as a paratrooper during WWII, landing behind enemy lines to set up communications. After the war, he worked as a telephone lineman. He was the man who climbed the telephone pole and repaired or maintained the transmission wiring. Then he worked as an aerospace engineering drafter for McDonnell Douglas Corporation (which later merged with Boeing), converting design specifications of aerospace engineers into detailed technical drawings that could be used in the manufacturing process. My Aunt Christine told me that he also worked for Lockheed Martin performing similar duties. While working in the aerospace industry, he attended night school to become a chiropractor and later set up practice in a shared building with another doctor.

Grandpa Rob often adjusted our backs when we needed it (especially my back, when I was sore from lifting kids on ponies all day at the farm). As he aged, he retired from the chiropractic field and kept busy as a courier and then finally a security guard. Grandpa Rob liked to dabble in different job fields and never stopped working. He had a great sense of humor, and I always felt very loved by him. He had a bright, thin-lipped smile. You knew he was happy when you saw that smile. He drove a white Cadillac with a license plate that read "Dr. Rob." When I was younger, I thought that was so cool. In hindsight, it's super cheesy to me! Grandpa Rob remarried again after Grandma Lorraine, only to divorce once again. He loved his fried steaks and living single after his third divorce. He got along well with my other grandparents and would often comment how he was going to "steal" my Grandma Sheila away from Grandpa Jack. He was a character. Growing up, I didn't spend as much time with my paternal grandparents as I did with my maternal grandparents, Grandpa Jack and Grandma Sheila; nonetheless, they were always truly special to me.

A few months into my research, I learned that Grandpa Jack and Grandma Sheila had a collection of 8mm film reels from the 1950s to 1960s and a projector. I asked Grandpa Jack if I could watch the videos, and he told me his projector didn't work but I could have the reels. I took them so that I could later figure out a way to convert them to DVD.

During my conversations with Grandpa Jack, I took notes and kept some of his pictures. As I learned new facts, I'd safely store the information in my new family history file. I took great care of the photographs, making copies and laminating them in case the originals faded or got destroyed somehow. I ended up interviewing Grandpa Jack on camera, too, so I could have a filmed version as a keepsake. It was such a treasure having Grandpa Jack's pictures and spending that time with him talking about Grandma Sheila and the family, especially because I was so close to them both.

A couple of years later, in 2002, I converted Grandpa Jack and Grandma Sheila's 8mm reels to DVD and watched them with Grandpa Jack and our whole nearby family. Afterward, I remember feeling very accomplished. I'd completed a huge project for myself and for the generations to come. All the research I'd gathered in my new file, as well as the pictures and reels, really honored the memories of my elders, and I could feel the pride radiating from Grandma Lorraine and Grandpa Jack when we spoke about their past. For me, too, gaining knowledge and being able to put faces and names on my biological family was truly a gift. It was my pride and joy to have all of this in my possession.

In October 2004 my dad got a phone call from Grandpa Rob's boss saying that my grandfather hadn't shown up for his shift as a security guard. He'd had a heart attack in his home and called 911. He was rushed to the hospital where he underwent quadruple bypass surgery, then developed pneumonia and was placed on a ventilator. His condition was grave, and the nurses were keeping him sedated most of the time. This was not long after I'd started dating Nathan, who came with me to the hospital to say my goodbyes. I'll never forget telling Grandpa Rob directly into his ear that Nathan and I were engaged to be married. He was in and out of consciousness, but after I whispered those words to him, his eyes opened up wide and he squeezed my hand. I'll always remember that moment of happiness he was able to convey to me as he exhausted his final reserves of energy. Grandpa Rob passed away two days after my birthday in the winter of 2004 before I could get started on his family history, something I regret to this day. You always think you have more time until you don't. However, I was grateful to have gathered a multitude of information from Grandma Lorraine at the time. And she filled me in on Grandpa Rob's family as much as she could.

After Grandpa Rob died in 2004, I paused my genealogy work to focus on finishing my degree. In between all of the researching and interviewing, and working full-time to pay for school, I'd graduated, gotten married, and given birth to two children, and we had moved at least five times. The years were flying by. My daughter was a year and a half old when Grandpa Jack passed away in February 2013, and by 2015, Nathan and I had moved

350 miles away from my family in Southern California, including Grandma Lorraine, who was the only grandparent I had left. I was so grateful that I'd gathered Grandpa Jack's information when he was still alive. With all the information from Grandma Lorraine and Grandpa Jack, my genealogy files felt complete . . . or so I thought.

CHAPTER TWO: DNA

JANUARY–FEBRUARY 2018

In 2017 all the hype on DNA testing was circulating throughout many of my friends and family members. Websites like Ancestry.com made it easy for people to research their genealogy—you didn't need to hire an expert anymore. Since these sites had started offering DNA testing services, several people I knew were doing tests and going on about their results and how fun it was to see precise percentages of their heritage. It seemed like a fun discovery! The kind of thing you could share with your family and then file away and move on. On New Year's Eve in 2017, Nathan and I decided to join the amusement. On January 1, 2018, we purchased a set of four DNA kits and thought we could give the extras to our parents if they wanted one. We imagined it would be entertaining to find out what a little bit of saliva had to say.

The kits arrived quickly and we eagerly opened them up, registered them online, read the instructions, and started spitting. Nathan's parents had already done a different test, so we held on to the two extras for the time being. I never thought for a single second that anything questionable would come back. After all, I already knew I was of Ukrainian, Ashkenazi Jewish, and

Syrian descent, as well as German and French. I just wanted to see percentages for each one of these. I couldn't wait to see if I was more Jewish or more German and how much French or Syrian I had. I knew where Grandpa Jack's family had immigrated from because Bonnie had given me that information, but I also wondered if I could find out where my dad's German and French sides came from.

Nearly six weeks had passed when, on February 12, 2018, at the age of thirty-nine, I received an email that my DNA results were ready. I was so excited I could hardly contain myself. I thought, *This is a fun Valentine's gift!* I quickly logged in and clicked the DNA tab at the top of the web page.

Little did I know that a quiet storm was brewing in the shadows. I had no idea what was coming when I clicked on that *DNA Results* button . . . My entire world was about to crash, and worse, someone very dear to me would be completely shattered.

To my great surprise, this is what came up:

- 25% Southern Italy
- 27% Ashkenazi Jewish (Ukraine/Austria areas)
- And the rest split between Germany, France, England, and the Baltics

Ashkenazi Jewish, German, French, yes. English and Baltic also made sense after learning more from my Grandma Lorraine. So that all seemed legit. However, Italian? . . . NO.

These results were very strange. Where did the Italian come from? And so much of it?! I'd never heard of anyone in our family being Italian. And where was the Syrian DNA? I had a million questions and doubts already. I started questioning the test's authenticity, purchased a 23andMe test, and immediately sent it in. My sister Rebecca told me she'd also decided to take a test, but her results were still pending. I was thrilled that we'd be able to compare and catch the error *my* test had made.

The annoyances of my "false test" subsided for the time being. Then a couple of weeks later, while waiting for my 23andMe results, Rebecca's DNA results arrived. She too shared a similar amount of Italian and 0 percent Syrian. We were so puzzled. How could this be? There had to be some sort of mix-up or error. My 23andMe results came back shortly following hers and had nearly the exact results as my Ancestry test! The Italian showed 25 percent and there was 0 percent Syrian or any form of Middle Eastern heritage. We weren't panicking; it just seemed weird. Okay, so now what?

I shared the news with my parents, and they were both shocked to hear of the results but also extremely curious to know where the Italian could have come from and why the Syrian DNA was mysteriously missing. I went back to the family history file I'd made seventeen years earlier after my interviews with Grandpa Jack, Grandma Lorraine, and Cousin Bonnie. I thought maybe Grandpa Jack had got his Syrian heritage wrong. But all of the information in my file verified the Syrian connection.

I then asked my parents if they'd consider taking the two extra tests we'd purchased. My dad's intrigue grew, and he was willing to test and became excited to learn more. My mom couldn't have cared less and said, "I know where I come from. I don't need to do a test." *Okay, fine,* I thought. I'd be happy to have my dad's side for now. At least we could see his exact heritage. But I put both test kits in the mail in case my mom changed her mind, which she did—they both ended up testing shortly after our conversation. Go figure.

So there I was, a year away from turning forty, with one living grandparent, Grandma Lorraine, who was currently in hospice care. I had to follow up with her on this immediately! I thought about what I would say when I called her. I remember thinking,

Do I even want to look into this? Is it even worth the effort? What good will this bring? What could I possibly discover that I didn't already know about my family? I already knew everything there was to know! Maybe this one tiny detail wouldn't be anything after all? Yet despite all these questions running through my mind, my curiosity was taking over.

I logged back in to my Ancestry account and saw that I had a notification informing me that I had new DNA matches. I was completely new to the Ancestry site, so I just mindlessly clicked on the *DNA Matches* button.

On the website, the DNA match list displays relatives who are biologically closest to you. I would've expected to see my parents at the top of my list, but their results hadn't come back yet. For the time being, aside from my sister, the following names I've never heard of before appeared as my *closest* genetic relatives:

- Maryann—Predicted relationship: first or second cousin
- James—Predicted relationship: first or second cousin
- Dana—Predicted relationship: first or second cousin

Who were these people?? I clicked on Maryann first. She was 100 percent Italian. I clicked on James next. He was 100 percent Italian. Then I clicked on Dana. She was 100 percent Italian, too.

This was so odd! Who were these closely related individuals who were 100 percent Italian? And *I* was 25 percent Italian?! Who in the world was Italian in our family (besides myself and Rebecca, as I'd just learned)?? I never considered that somewhere in all of this, someone had been dishonest, or that what I'd taken for granted as the truth might actually not be true at all.

As far as I could remember in 2018, I couldn't tell whether my DNA matches had come from the maternal or paternal side of my family on the Ancestry website. So it was a murky guessing game at that point. I kept wondering how and where in the world these three people might fit into my family. Our family had always been very close, and I'd never heard these names before. Nor did their pictures look familiar.

I sat in my office for a few minutes staring at the names, then decided to call Rebecca. I told her how I'd been matched to three Italian cousins. "It's *so* weird!" I said. "I have no idea who these people are!"

Rebecca immediately logged in to her account to see if they showed up on her side, too. And they did!

"We should ask Mom and Dad if they recognize these names," she said.

I volunteered to make the call, and Mom's response was the same as Rebecca's. "I have no idea who they are!" she said. My dad hadn't heard of them either. He added that his family also wasn't Italian. "I don't see how they could be related," he said.

We were all confused, but we all felt the same about one thing: we wanted to know what was up! My parents supported the idea of reaching out to these newfound family members.

"Is there a way to get in touch and ask them how they're related to you?" Mom asked.

I looked around the Ancestry website where it showed the matched relatives and saw there was an option to send them a message.

With all of us in agreement, I went ahead and messaged the three Italians to ask how they could be related to us. And I patiently waited for a response.

CHAPTER THREE: INTERFAITH LOVE

My mother, Michelle, was born in 1954 at Terrace Heights Hospital in Queens to my grandparents, Jack and Sheila. Since she was a little girl, Mom's nickname has been "Gabby," given to her by her father because she was always "jabbering," he once said. Mom retired in 2017 and now leads a couple social groups that focus on family relationships. She spends a lot of time reading and listening to stories of hardship, and she enjoys being an ear for people.

My mother is the middle child of two brothers. Though she didn't play sports when she was younger, she was a Girl Scout in a troop led by her mother, with whom she was very close. There was a story repeated among her family members about how she would constantly "terrorize" her cousin, who was one year younger than her. Once Mom put a water hose in her cousin's mouth and turned it on. I often heard them talking about this during family visits, and my mother would just laugh in embarrassment alongside everyone else. I could never picture Mom being a rebellious child like they described, and in her defense, her cousin said she'd gone along with it! To me, Mom's so-called terrorizing sounded more like the typical pranks kids would play.

Then again, children in the 1950s were meant to be perfectly behaved. Girls especially, were expected to be obedient, modest, and well-mannered, so I guess she broke that mold.

After my mom and her brothers were uprooted from New York to California in 1970, she attended Van Nuys High School, but she retained her New York accent, especially when around her family. The move was tough on her, and she kept to herself a lot of the time. At seventeen she graduated and began attending a local community college, later becoming a pharmacy technician, her job until she retired, and she can tell you about any medication.

My mother is Jewish. When she was eighteen, her older brother Steven introduced her to the Lord. She ended up getting baptized in a Christian church, and her father, my Grandpa Jack, immediately kicked her out of her home for "abandoning her faith." However, my mother will tell you that she did not convert. "I *am* and always *will be* Jewish," she says. She just chose to *expand* her faith. According to my mother, Grandma Sheila didn't want her to leave. She missed her at home. She and my mother even worked together at Milton's Pharmacy at the time. Almost a year after my mother's eviction, Grandma Sheila was able to convince Grandpa Jack to let her come back home. It wouldn't be for long though. My mother had already begun to date my father, who was Christian, before moving back in with her parents at the age of nineteen.

When I was five years old, my parents bought their first home. It was a very small, three-bedroom, one-bathroom home in Reseda, California. Three girls and one bathroom—my poor dad! My mom had the top priority of that bathroom every morning before work. It was a small home, but it was our home. My parents lived there for thirty-four years. As we got older, my mom assigned weekly chores to my sister and me, and it was our job to keep up with these contributions, especially considering all the pets we had: one cat, two dogs, two rabbits, one rat, one lizard, and a duck. I remember spilling her nail polish remover on the wooden coffee table once and trying to cover up the damage with her magazines, but even though I was petrified, my mother never yelled at me.

Mom always loved the sun and tans well (sadly, I didn't inherit that gift). She also loves being near water—sitting by a pool or on the beach. When we were younger, during our summer breaks, whenever we weren't splashing around in my grandparents' pool, she'd take Ana, my sister, and me to Zuma Beach off Pacific Coast Highway in Malibu. It was the highlight of summer for me. I almost always fell asleep in her Mazda 626 on the ride home listening to Anita Baker or Luther Vandross while being stuck in traffic on the 101 Freeway.

If not her tanning ability, I did inherit her love of music. And we both love horses. I have very fond memories of riding with her and just wish we had some pictures!

On occasion, Mom would borrow a horse named Tonka from my friend and join me for trail rides. Tonka was a very mellow Pinto, about fourteen years old at the time, and he got along well with my horse Stormy.

I always rode bareback because that was how Ana and I learned and had always ridden on the farm. My mom was not an experienced rider and understandably wasn't comfortable riding without a saddle. Also, when she was around six or seven years old, she was thrown off a horse, so having a saddle helped her feel a little more secure, she said. Tonka was wonderful for her. We often reminisce about riding the Chatsworth Park trails together. Mom recalls the quiet she felt while riding Tonka. "I remember peaceful, warm, sunny days and wide-open spaces. Surrounded by nature, it was like time didn't matter," she said.

I admire that my mom never bad-mouths anyone, and I only saw her truly angry a handful of times in my life. It takes a great deal to upset her, so if you were one of the *lucky* few who felt her wrath, it must have been warranted, because my mom is not a mean-spirited person. She treats everyone with respect and kindness and maintains a high standard of morals. She is not an affectionate, mushy person. But you feel her love through her immense loyalty, dependability, honesty, and caring nature, and the fact that she will always show up for you. She is always true to her word. What you see is what you get. When Mom found out I was talking too much in my social studies class instead of doing my work, she showed up and sat in my classroom. Mr. Moore must have been in on it because he had a chair ready for her. At first, I was embarrassed, but later realized that's who she is. She will always show up. There is no doubt how much she loves her family. She truly is a wonderful mother and human, and she loves the Lord.

My father, Robert, was born at Wesley Memorial Hospital in Chicago, Illinois, in 1952 to Robert and Lorraine. The oldest of four children, he has a younger brother and two younger sisters. Dad's family moved to California when he was young, and he grew up in Reseda, attending a Catholic private school and church. He didn't play sports but loved working on cars and building things. He has a mechanical mind. After high school, he was enlisted as a marine, but he got discharged a few months later after a knee injury that required surgery later in life.

My father started attending Church on the Way in Van Nuys in 1972, which was led by Pastor Jack Hayford, and that's where he met my mother. She had also been attending with her older brother, and they were in a college group together. She asked him out for a coffee, and after about a year of dating, he planned to ask her to marry him. My Grandpa Rob initially discouraged the marriage to my mother because she was Jewish, but ultimately ended up supporting my father's decision.

I remember Dad telling me about the proposal when I was in my twenties. Mom was back living with her parents after being kicked out and working at Milton's Pharmacy at the time, Dad said. They'd just gotten back from a church function. It was nighttime, and they were sitting in front of her apartment in Dad's red-and-white Pontiac Tempest.

He said to her, "What would you say if I asked you to marry me?"

She answered, "I would say yes."

"So I'm asking."

"So I'm answering."

And that was that, my dad said.

Now, he just needed her parents' permission to officially marry her.

Dad told me how he, my mom, and her parents went to a Russian restaurant called Moskva Cliff in Studio City. Her parents had known what was coming with the dinner, Dad said.

"Your grandmother was just sitting there smiling, and your grandfather looked at me and said, 'Nu??'" Which was my grandfather's term for "What's up? Spit it out. What's new or what do you want?"

"I was so nervous that before we even ordered the food, I reached across the table, took your grandfather's Scotch, and downed it. Your grandfather's eyes got big. He wasn't amused. Your grandmother was laughing, though, because they both knew the reason we were at the dinner and how nervous I was. That didn't stop your grandfather from being a ball-breaker with me," Dad said. "Ball-breaker" was a term my dad often used to describe Grandpa Jack.

He continued. "Finally, I said, 'I'm asking permission to marry your daughter.' Your grandmother was so happy, she had a huge smile, and to my surprise, your grandfather just said, 'Okay.'"

The next day, my newly engaged parents were driving on the 101 Freeway near Studio City. They were in his Pontiac when suddenly Dad attempted to merge to get on the 405 and the car spun out, ending up on the wrong side of the freeway facing oncoming traffic. Thankfully, there were no cars in sight at that moment except for one with a lady inside who looked at them with huge eyes after what she'd just witnessed. She and Dad exchanged looks before he quickly turned the car around, got onto the correct side of the road, and drove off. They were very shaken.

"There were definitely angels watching over us that afternoon," Dad said.

He went on to tell me how Grandma Sheila had been like a mother to him.

"She was always loving and caring toward me. When I was sick and hospitalized, your grandma came and sat by my side every day. She said she wasn't leaving until she knew I'd be okay. Another time, as I was walking in your grandparents' front door to visit your mom, Sheila said, 'Stop right there.' Then she walked up to me with a pair of scissors and trimmed my mustache. When she finished, she smiled and said, 'There, now you're handsome,' and gave me a hug. She always treated me with love."

My mother was nineteen and my father was twenty-one when my Grandpa Jack and Grandma Sheila gave her away for marriage at Church on the Way. Grandpa Jack grew increasingly accepting and supportive of my mom's participation in the church, which led him and Grandma Sheila to frequently attend church events, particularly when Mom sang in the choir.

My parents first moved into an apartment that was close to Milton's Pharmacy before settling into the home where they raised Rebecca and me.

Dad would occasionally lose his temper with my sister and me, but this was mostly when we were little kids and doing dumb things like accidentally breaking the glass window on our front door. I'd say his irritation was justified. (It was actually Dad who got mad at me for spilling nail polish remover on the wooden table, not Mom.)

When I was about five, my dad began operating his own pool company. He would wake up my sister and me at five in the morning to go on his pool route. It was still dark outside, and we were often half asleep when we climbed into his truck.

"C'mon, let's go," he'd say. "When we're done, we'll go get a doughnut." My sister and I helped him net the pools and check the chemical levels. We loved putting the droplets in the tube and watching the colors change. Our favorite house was one we called "the jungle house." We felt like we were in a lush Amazonian rainforest while exploring the backyard of that house. The low-lying palm branches brushed the tops of our heads as we ran underneath them, and there were Birds of Paradise all around. The sound of water falling over rocks into the pool made it feel like we were right next to a real waterfall deep in the forest. And each day, after finishing work, Dad kept his word and we ended up at Yum Rich Donuts on Vanowen Street. It was such a treat!

The pool business was his day job, and at night he worked at the neighborhood hardware store called Ole's, later named Builders Emporium. I used to go with him to pick up his paychecks, and I memorized his employee number after hearing him give it to the lady behind the desk: 102128. I don't know why I still know it, but I do.

Back then, Dad drove a small burgundy Toyota pickup truck that was eventually stolen from the parking lot of the hardware store. I was home with my mother when he called about his truck going missing. I still remember her response while she held the phone, "What?! You're kidding! Okay, we'll come pick you up."

Shortly after this, my dad ended his pool business to go back to work for the City of Los Angeles, as he had in the years following his military discharge, as a gardener, and finally as a supervisor. I was still too young to be left home alone during summer break, so I would go to the park with him. I loved being at the same location where Dad was working. I knew all his coworkers and employees, and I always felt safe. I attended the summer day camps for free, and later during high school, I became a camp counselor. The park was near Grandpa Jack's apartment, and sometimes I would visit him after camp finished.

When I worked at the pony-rides farm, Dad would drive me and the neighborhood kids to and from work on the weekends. Five or six kids would pile in the back of his new Mazda pickup truck at 7 a.m. on Saturdays. After I quit working at the pony rides, he drove me to my jobs at the local Swap Meet and Designer Labels for Less until he taught me how to drive a stick shift and I got my license. I remember him telling me, "You can drive anything if you can drive a stick, so you have to learn."

I've always admired how hardworking and kind he was. My father has a very warm heart. He loves to help other people, and when I was growing up, he prayed with me every night before bed. I remember how he would hold my hair over the toilet when I was sick and pray with me afterward and also when I had nightmares. When pages of my senior yearbook were torn by some jerk, Dad took it without me knowing, taped the pages of the whole book, and silently gave it back to me. I was so taken aback by this. He was always so thoughtful, caring, and nurturing. That's the kind of man he is.

As my grandparents got older, Dad often helped them with home repairs or running errands. He also dedicated Sundays to volunteering at a smaller church we started attending when I was about eight years old, called Fountain Springs Fellowship. As a teenager, I became a member of the youth group and shared countless adventures with my church family. One day, my parents received the heartbreaking news that our Pastor was involved in an affair with the church secretary. This revelation shattered our church community and forced my parents to leave Fountain Springs and go back to Church on the Way. It was devastating for me, as I cherished my time in the youth group during my teenage years. Regrettably, I did not join another youth group after that.

In 2008, after thirty-two dedicated years with the City of Los Angeles, Dad retired. He then became a Reseda Neighborhood Council member and served on various committees. He also volunteered at Kaiser Hospital a few times a week. Selflessly, for forty hours per week, he helped take care of Grandma Lorraine, who wasn't able to be home unattended, until she passed away. My father loves to serve, loves his family, and most of all, like my mother, he loves the Lord.

To say I've been lucky to have such wonderful parents is an understatement. Their unwavering reliance on the Lord and each other significantly facilitated my ability to navigate the uncertainties I would soon face.

CHAPTER FOUR: THE SIMPLEST ANSWER

FEBRUARY 2018

While my family and I patiently awaited responses from my new Italian cousins and for my parents' DNA to come back, I decided to call Cousin Bonnie again. She knew all about Grandpa Jack's family history and said she had no knowledge of anyone Italian but that I should let her know what I found out. More confused than ever, I called my Grandma Lorraine. She was nearing ninety and on hospice care but still had all her wits about her. She was considering doing a DNA test herself, and I fully trusted whatever information she could give me. On the call, I told her how my test had come up 25 percent Italian and asked if there was any Italian on her side of the family or on Grandpa Rob's side. She immediately answered with full certainty and confidence, "No, the Italian is *not* from our side."

Back to square one. Jewish, Syrian, German, French . . . I didn't get it.

Then a few days later, I got an email notification from Ancestry.com. Straightaway, I logged in and found a message from Maryann.

"I am looking for a first cousin (female)," she wrote, "born in NYC around 1950."

My head started spinning. I read it again. And again. And again. I couldn't process what I was reading. Then it hit me like a ton of bricks.

My mother was born in 1954 in New York!

I immediately called my sister to tell her about the message and asked her whether or not she thought this could be about our mom. I was standing in the kitchen, leaning over the granite countertop with the phone held firmly to my ear. My husband Nathan was next to me, listening in as my sister and I discussed all the possibilities, coming up with increasingly outrageous and illogical hypotheticals as we tried to figure out how these people could *possibly* be related to our mother. Maybe during the war our ancestors' DNA got intermingled somehow? Or maybe Grandpa Jack was Italian and didn't know it, and Bonnie's information—years of research— was wrong?

Nathan can be a man of few words, and he doesn't involve himself in family ordeals. Ever. But halfway through these far-out theories, he intervened. He gently grabbed both of my shoulders, moving me away from the countertop, looked me in the eye, and said the words I'll never forget:

"Sharon, sometimes the simplest answer *is* the answer." He paused for a moment, then continued, "One of your grandparents is not your grandparent."

Rebecca and I were completely spellbound and speechless by his words as I held the phone to my ear. He was still holding me and trying to relay this as gently as he could. It must have been hard for him. Nathan is not impulsive or irrational. He's a keen listener with a very strong moral compass, and he always acts with integrity and sensitivity toward others. He wasn't speaking impulsively or saying this to be cruel. He was saying it to open our eyes, to tenderly guide us to the truth. I can't express now how much I appreciated his honesty at that moment. And yet, even though I knew what Nathan said was probably right, for some reason I went into defense mode. Still holding the phone to my ear, I just stared at him. "Huh? Absolutely not! That can't be! Rebecca, do you think . . . ?"

But the more Nathan's words sank in, the more reasonable they seemed and the less defense I had against them.

After saying goodbye to my sister, Nathan watched me as I began pacing the kitchen. I knew that look. I couldn't lift my head to face him. To face this potential truth. He wanted me to consider things rationally, but he also knew I needed to process things, and he understood the fragility of my emotions around what was happening. He stood completely still and waited until I'd finally stopped pacing.

"Sharon, think about it. I'm just saying, it seems pretty obvious to me given how closely related you are to the Italians . . . and you're both 25 percent Italian. It's the only scenario that seems possible," he said.

Then my heart started pounding as I considered that maybe he was right. *But I don't want him to be right! My grandparents are my grandparents: Lorraine and Rob—Sheila and Jack!*

I knew my parents' DNA tests were in progress, so there was no stopping this train. It never crossed my mind to walk away at that moment or trouble my mom with this information because I was still holding on to the hope that maybe it had nothing to do with her. I'd recently been contacted by another cousin named Patti, whom I'd never heard of before, and she said she was looking for her birth father. Maybe this had something to do with her?

Over the next few hours, as I processed Nathan's words, my children were a great distraction, keeping me from spiraling as I helped them with math homework and reading followed by cooking dinner, bathing, and getting them off to bed. But once the house was quiet, I gathered myself, went to my office, and wrote back to Maryann as well as Dana and James, asking for clarification or if they'd be willing to talk off of Ancestry. I added my phone number and email at the end of the message. Dana replied straightaway, offering to call me and give me their side of the story.

CHAPTER FIVE: JACK

"When I first met your grandmother, she was a beautiful, witty, well-dressed dancer and singer with a heart of gold. That's how I remember her."

It was early 2000. I was twenty-two years old and officially interviewing my Grandpa Jack, who was seventy-seven. My friend, who was a film student at the time, agreed to help me convert all of Grandpa Jack and Grandma Sheila's 8mm video reels to DVD. Years' worth of family moments, such as my mom and grandmother on the beach together, my mom's birthday parties, family trips, and the three children playing in the yard. My friend's mother had come along to help me film the interview. She had a professional camera, with much better quality than the home camcorder I owned. I planned to keep Grandpa Jack's interview for my genealogy records alongside his 8mm video reels, which we would convert. My friend would also do the editing and add in my choices of music. A mixture of older and modern-day songs like "Diamond Road" by Sheryl Crow, "I Can't Help Myself (Sugar Pie, Honey Bunch)" by the Four Tops, and "Zing Went the Strings of My Heart" by Judy Garland were pulled from my CD collection at the time. Then I would make enough copies of the DVD for the whole family to keep.

That afternoon, we were at Grandpa Jack's studio apartment in Tarzana, California, in his living room. Grandpa Jack met us in the parking lot and walked us through the stairwell to get to his front door. His smile beamed as he opened the door, and I could tell he was as excited as I was to see this family project coming to life, because the minute we walked through the door, Grandpa Jack immediately began naming everyone in the collage of pictures hanging on his wall. My videographer stood close to both of us to film the photos he was describing. After a while, he offered us a drink and then settled across from us in his blue recliner chair, which had a $100 money blanket draped over the back.

From where we were sitting, I could see Grandpa Jack's kitchen to the left, and behind his recliner was his bedroom, which contained a glossy brown wooden dresser, a nightstand, and a meticulously made king-size bed. Above the bed hung a painting of a dark-haired, naked woman lying on her side, partially propped up on her arms. Her pose is sexy, with her eyes closed and her arms mostly covering her breasts. There's a twisted piece of white fabric draped in an S-curve from her waist to her groin area. As a kid, I used to think the painting was so weird and that the fabric was a snake. To be honest, it used to creep me out. Grandpa Jack told me he'd bought it years ago because the woman looked like Grandma Sheila. After hearing that, I agreed they did look kind of alike, though I still thought it was a weird painting.

Along with our drinks, Grandpa Jack had filled his large square green ceramic tray with pistachios. I remembered seeing both the tray and the coffee table in all his homes, which I'd visited growing up.

As I began the interview, he was chewing gum as he began to speak. I remember thinking later that I should have had him spit that out before the interview!

It was my first official sit-down with him, and I had my file with my own and my cousin Bonnie's notes and photos spread out on the coffee table between us, along with the collage, which he'd taken down from the wall. As we talked, Grandpa Jack commented on the pictures, filling in details from his memory and pointing out people and how we were related. He also had a small pile of loose photographs of his siblings and his mother Zakiah, whom he was so happy to tell me about. There were also a few photos of my grandmother, including some I hadn't seen before, like the one that had prompted his comment about her being a singer and dancer. With a big smile, Grandpa Jack slid an eight-by-ten-inch black-and-white photo from a manila envelope taken in the early 1940s. The photo shows Grandma Sheila on the floor, propped up on her elbows covered by long velvet gloves, legs extended in front of her, in a pose that makes me think of a synchronized swimmer doing scissor kicks. She's wearing a dress patterned in sequined polka dots with a strapless, heart-shaped bodice and a full skirt forming a circle around her on the floor, showing off shapely legs in fishnet stockings and shiny patent-leather heels with ankle buckles. Her hair is teased into a bouffant, her brows dramatically arched, and she has a full-toothed smile. She is warm and magnetic. It was hard to believe that this was my grandmother!

Grandpa Jack told me Grandma Sheila had gone on the road dancing with her older sister—my grandaunt, Paula ("Aunt Paula")—before they met in 1946. I was in a trance listening to him as he looked down at the picture in his hand and said, "She was so talented, and she had such a beautiful voice. She could have been the next Eve Arden, Ethel Merman, or Judy Garland!" I'd always known Grandma Sheila could sing very well—everyone in our family did. I also knew she'd been a dancer over the years, but I never asked what kind of dancer.

"We were young newlyweds, and I was in love with her, what can I say?" Grandpa Jack continued. "We were young, she was talented, and I was proud of her. There was also the hope between us that she could make it to film, but she gave it all up to raise a family."

At the time, this all seemed very reasonable to me, though years later, I wish I'd asked him more. Listening to Grandpa Jack talk about my grandmother that day, I noticed, as I had often before, the way his face lit up. I'd always loved the way he talked about her. It was as if she could do no wrong. He put her on a pedestal, and you could tell how much he adored her. I was so young when Grandma Sheila died, so listening to him helped me learn things about her that I never got to hear straight from her.

That day, I was seeing a different side of Grandpa Jack, too. In addition to the Grandpa Jack I knew from my childhood, there would be many other Jacks I'd find out about throughout our interviews. There'd be enough to fill a whole book about him. He was one of those people who had lived many lives.

Grandpa Jack was my maternal grandfather, and his Sephardic Jewish family had immigrated from Syria to New York, where he was born in 1923. He was the fifth of eight full siblings and had two older half-siblings. His father Murad (Max), who was thirty years older than his mother Zakiah (Sadie), ran some imports and exports with his older sons and was also a candy peddler. Max died when Grandpa Jack was only five years old. When Grandpa Jack was about six years old, he and his two siblings were enlisted in a Hebrew orphanage for six months before returning home with their mother Sadie. He didn't share this detail with me directly, or with anyone in the family that I'm aware of—I found this on my own while researching family records online. But I've often wondered about all the ways those months in the orphanage must have affected him, including his view of what made a family, biological or not.

Growing up, I always loved visiting my grandparents at their home in Encino, California. My earliest memories of Grandpa Jack were his stern voice and thick New York accent, and especially his smile, which lit up the room, and the wet kisses he gave us on our cheeks. I also remember the way he would softly squeeze my cheek between his index and middle fingers, or cup my face with his soft hand. He wasn't always tender with me, though. I remember him spanking me when I was young, and Grandma Sheila would yell, "Bessbeh!" at him. (I still don't know what language that word comes from, or what it means exactly, but I imagined it was her way of saying, "Knock it off!" or "Stop it!")

Grandpa Jack demanded respect. When he spoke, you better be listening. It was Grandpa Jack who had kicked my mom out of the house for getting baptized, but then welcomed her back because, above all else, he loved her dearly, regardless of her religious choices.

He smoked TRUE Blue cigarettes, dressed well, and kept his nails manicured. He kept Klondike bars in his freezer and always had a wad of cash in his pocket. Every holiday he would pull it out and give us money, and I used to think he must be very rich! He started calling me "Shorty" when I was just a kid, and honestly, I can't remember him ever using my actual name. I have fond memories of my sister and me searching for the hidden matzah at Passover every year, lighting candles, and opening presents at Hanukkah. We spent our childhood weekends swimming in my grandparents' pool followed by dinners. The after-dinner delight was watching Grandpa Jack peel apples with a paring knife in one long peel, a skill I adopted and still do to this day. A peeled apple was our cherished dessert followed by the occasional green Jell-O topped with whipped cream that Grandma Sheila would make for us. I remember falling asleep on the car ride home from their house even though they lived only a couple miles away.

This didn't change, even after Grandma Sheila passed away in 1991 and Grandpa Jack moved in with her older sister, my Aunt

Paula, who was a widow. They co-rented a townhome about fifteen minutes away from his previous home. Aunt Paula and Grandpa Jack lived together for a few years until she moved out of state. They seemed like good roommates for each other, and I can imagine living with her made Grandpa Jack feel closer to Grandma Sheila. Aunt Paula was sassy and still glamorous in her way, even when she grew older. She was always kind to me, and I really loved being around her. In their townhome she occupied the master suite with the huge bathroom and vanity mirrors, which seemed fitting for a diva like my Aunt Paula. Grandpa Jack had the smaller bedroom, but he didn't seem to mind.

We often visited Aunt Paula and Grandpa Jack for dinner, and their townhome community also had a pool. Like when Grandma Sheila was alive, we often had family get-togethers at their house. In addition to his peeling skills, Grandpa Jack was a fantastic cook. His homemade french fries and latkes were a thrill for us to enjoy. We also loved his spinach pie—a dish my mother adopted and often made for us, and still does to this day. After dinner, my sister and I learned to play Rummikub with Aunt Paula and Grandpa Jack. It was a family favorite. The room would break out in friendly arguments and laughs whenever someone else joined and "messed up the board." It was hilarious, and I'll always treasure those days.

In addition to being a devoted grandfather and master chef, Grandpa Jack had many other attributes. He spoke Arabic fluently and a few words of Yiddish, such as *Behaimeh*, which he jokingly used to call my dad when he was annoyed. Unfortunately, Grandpa Jack also liked to gamble a lot. He had several connections to people in Las Vegas and would always stay at the Tropicana Hotel when he visited. When my mother was pregnant with me in 1978, the family took a trip to Las Vegas. I would be named the "Lucky Baby" afterward, because on that trip, Grandpa Jack rubbed my mom's belly for good luck on a bet. And he won BIG—$30,000 big! It was a story that was repeated to me over my childhood. I have to admit, it always made me feel a little special. But gambling didn't always go his way. This habit later cost him and Grandma Sheila their family home in Rosedale in 1969. I went to Las Vegas with him when I was in my twenties, but I was naive about any of his dealings at the time.

Grandpa Jack

Then there was "Jack, the courageous war hero." We had talked about his military service in the U.S. Army during World War II, which earned him both a Purple Heart and a Bronze Star medal, among other awards for his bravery and service. There was a thin line that ran halfway around the outside of his upper right arm, a scar where his arm was nearly severed after being shot. He also had a smaller, sunken scar on the inside of his wrist where he caught shrapnel, which his watch usually covered. Still, I clearly remember both scars, especially the bigger one, though as a child, I never understood the depth of what they meant. Grandpa Jack had seen and experienced things I could never imagine—growing up during the Depression with very little food, losing his father, being separated from his mother and living in an orphanage, going to war and being fully immersed in chaos, including getting shot and watching all his friends get blown up. Yet he was full of love for us.

Throughout my life, I could always feel Grandpa Jack's adoration for his family, especially his children and his grandchildren. Listening to him talk about them was truly a cherished time for both of us, especially when he talked about my mom, his one and only beloved daughter. The two of them were always very close. Grandpa Jack and I were very close, too. I saw him so often that it felt as if he somewhat raised my sister and me. He also lived with us for a couple of years when I was about seventeen until he moved back into his own apartment. I am so grateful I got to dance with him at my wedding and have him at the hospital for the births of my children before he died. He also helped pray the blessing over the challah bread during my wedding reception, which Nathan and I incorporated to honor my Jewish heritage. Writing this now, I wish I had more time with him. I still have so many questions.

One thing that was never in question over the years was his love for my grandmother. That afternoon in Grandpa Jack's living room, I asked him about the day they first met. He went through his stack of family photos and showed me an older picture of them together in bathing suits. My mouth dropped seeing how young they looked.

"It was 1946," Grandpa Jack said. "I was at the swimming pool on Coney Island, and she was splashing my nephew. I said to her: 'What are you picking on him for? Come pick on me!' And then I dove in after her. The rest is history." He smiled that smile of his that lit up the room and always warmed my heart. He told me he asked her out that evening, and when he picked her up, he was blown away by her.

"When she opened the door, I said, 'Whoa!' because she looked so beautiful and she had—" His eyes widened as he motioned his two hands cupping two breasts over his chest, making me laugh, and my videographer suppressed a chuckle from behind the camera. "We dated for about a year and then got married."

Grandpa Jack said he got along well with Grandma Sheila's family, especially her sisters, Jean and Paula. He met her younger sister Jean at Steeplechase Park on Coney Island when she joined them one afternoon. Later, when I mentioned this conversation to Aunt Jean, she told me that Grandma Sheila had been trying to set her up with a boyfriend. Aunt Jean wasn't interested but went along so she could meet Grandpa Jack. While at Coney Island together, Grandma Sheila and Grandpa Jack went on the new "Parachute Jump" ride where two people sit together and you're taken 250 feet up in the air and then let go—to simulate jumping in a parachute. Aunt Jean later told me that the ride malfunctioned and my grandparents got stuck up there together. The emergency response team had to be called to assist in getting them down.

I asked Grandpa Jack how he had proposed to my grandmother.

"I said: 'You wanna get married?' And she said '*Yes!*'" He raised the pitch of his voice to sound like a woman and started smiling and laughing again. Then he got serious and held up his hand, pointing his index finger up in the air and saying, "But I told her, if we do, we have to move to California . . . I'd been there before, during my time in the army, and I wanted to go back. She agreed. So in 1947 we got on a bus that was going to Los Angeles and got married at a courthouse in Boyle Heights. We got two witnesses off the street and a rabbi."

I pictured Grandpa Jack approaching people on the street and saying, "Hey, do me a favor, would ya? I need two witnesses so I can marry that beautiful woman over there . . ." Then he would pull out his wad of cash and slip them a bill or two with a huge smile. He showed me a picture of them on their wedding day. They both had bright smiles. Funny, I saw this picture often but never realized it was their wedding photo because they are in day clothes instead of the typical wedding gown and formal suit. The fuzzy black-and-white photograph shows Grandpa Jack on the right side in a dark suit and tie and Grandma Sheila in a light-colored blouse and matching skirt. Grandpa Jack has his right arm around Grandma Sheila's waist, and her right hand is lovingly on top of his.

"And where did you live?" I asked.

"I was getting a pension from the army from being injured, so we bought a home in Encino for $10,000! We had no furniture, just a big empty house. So we went to a furniture store and bought a whole house of furniture. Then your Uncle Steven was born. So there we were . . . We got a house, a car, a dog, and a kid!" he said in a louder voice, eyebrows raised and with a smile of enthusiasm.

Grandpa Jack continued, "But then your grandmother started crying. 'I wanna go home and share him [Steven] with my family,' she said. I told her, 'Your family is here! I'm your family!' But what could I do? So we packed up and moved back to New York, and we ended up buying a brand-new house in Rosedale, and your Aunt Jean and Uncle Eddie bought the house next door to us. Then your mother came along and then your uncle."

AUTUMN LEAVES

Jack and Sheila in Rosedale, circa 1950

That day, as we wrapped up the interview, I took back the photos that Grandpa Jack gave me for my family files. When I look at them now and reflect on the interview, I notice things that don't quite add up, but which I couldn't have been aware of then. What would I have thought that day, listening to Grandpa Jack talk about my grandmother and their life together, knowing what I know now?

Not long after our interview, he moved in with a woman named Dorothy who lived next door to him in his apartment building. It was financially beneficial for both of them. She was a single woman with no children and just a little older than my mother. She was kind, gentle, and soft-spoken and took great care of Grandpa Jack as he was aging. Dorothy worked in a grocery store, and during her time off they played cards, cooked meals, and ran errands. It was good for him to have companionship, and he really cherished her. They lived together for over ten years. He nicknamed her "Cookie."

In the last year of Grandpa Jack's life, I lived an hour away and sadly didn't get to sit at his bedside and say my goodbyes in person. It was after 10 p.m. when my sister called me and held the phone to his ear so I could talk to him and say my goodbyes. Grandpa Jack lived until the age of eighty-nine, passing away of natural causes in 2013 in the apartment where he and Cookie lived.

There are so many ways to know someone, and each person has many layers to who they are and what makes them unique. One thing I think everyone could agree on is Grandpa Jack's capacity to love, right up to the end.

CHAPTER SIX: SHEILA

At the end of every phone call, Grandma Sheila would always say, "I love you." These are the memories that stay with you, as strong as any photo or keepsake. In the end, they're all you have. Still, I'll always wish we had more time together, more memories.

I adored Grandma Sheila. I loved her smile, I loved her laugh, and I loved the way she dressed and her big hair. She was always nurturing and patient, always speaking tenderly toward my sister Rebecca and me. During the summer, she would frequently swim with us and treat us to a Vienna Fingers cookie after a long day in her "hat-shaped" pool. She often went on walks to stay in shape, and she had the best jewelry, which I loved to look at and try on, if she let me. She often wore a gold fish necklace, but my favorite piece was her diamond heart-shaped necklace. Rebecca and I begged her to paint our nails, which she called "shovels" when they got too long, unlike hers, which were perfectly trimmed and painted. She had coloring books and *The Wizard of Oz* and Jane Fonda VHS tapes that we watched when we needed some downtime. We would sit quietly in the den on the blue sofas and zone out until our parents were ready to leave. My favorite meal she made was brisket and *keskasoon*, a traditional Syrian Jewish dish made with tiny pasta and chickpeas, followed by her green Jell-O for dessert that was prepared in individual crystal bowls. She would top each bowl with whipped cream. I always got excited to see our dessert prepared and waiting for us in her refrigerator. She gave the best hugs, and she never got mad. I loved the way she loved us.

Grandma Sheila

When I lost that love, it felt like the world as I knew it had ended. I was eleven years old when Grandma Sheila was diagnosed with stage 4 T-cell lymphoma in the summer of 1990. At first, I felt mostly confused—on the one hand she seemed "well" and was still herself, while on the other she lost most of her hair after beginning chemotherapy. I didn't understand what was going on, but seeing her with a wig, smiling and eating dinner with us on the weekends, reassured me that she was okay. I kept my mind busy at the pony-rides farm and writing poems. It helped, putting down the things I was feeling but couldn't fully understand. I would sit in my room with a spiral notebook and blue pen and just let everything pour out of me onto the paper. I wrote a couple of rhyming poems about her when she was still healthy.

Then, a few months later, in the winter of that year, Grandma Sheila wasn't okay. Her cancer was completely taking over, at a rapid pace. She stopped wearing her wigs or putting on makeup, and she stopped painting her nails. She wasn't eating much, and she became very frail. She still said, "I love you," but now in a fragile, shaky voice. My dear grandma was declining before my eyes, and I was completely heartbroken.

The last memory I have of her was the day I went to say goodbye. She was in the hospice bed in my grandparents' living room. She was wearing a white terry-cloth turban on her head. She was pale, very skinny, and barely alert. There was a window behind her bed, which was propped up so that she faced the living room where everyone sat on the tan sofas just next to the dining area and kitchen. From what I remember, my parents, Grandpa Jack, my younger uncle, and my grandaunt, Barbara, were there. My sister wasn't. She chose not to come and said it was because she didn't want to remember Grandma "that way." She preferred to remember our grandmother when she was vibrant and lively, not when she was fading away. To this day, she has no regrets about her choice.

The air was heavy with sadness, and everyone was crying, including me. I remember feeling very hot, too. I didn't know at the time, because I was so young, but it was because of all the crying. The hospice nurse said something like, "This is it." She counted down the blood pressure numbers as they slowly dropped, and my grandmother faded away as we gathered around her bed to say our goodbyes. Barbara held Grandma Sheila's hand and was sobbing uncontrollably. I remember seeing Grandpa Jack standing in the doorway facing outside and leaning his head against the wall in heartbreak after they took her body away.

I was in sixth grade and couldn't process why at the age of sixty-eight, my grandmother had to go. I was so distraught and felt like my whole world had come crashing down. One of my teachers, Mrs. Williams, wrote me the most heartfelt sympathy card. It touched my heart to know that one of my teachers *saw* me and what I was going through. Out of six teachers, she was the only one who did. I know secondary teachers have a lot on their plate, especially in today's teaching world. But I'll never forget her effort. It's these small acts of kindness that stay with you, like Grandma Sheila's hugs and "I love yous." I wish I still had Mrs. Williams's card.

At twelve, I had been too young to think of asking my grandmother about her life, but over the years I've learned more about her from cousins, my mother, and Grandpa Jack, and especially from Grandma Sheila's younger sister, Jean ("Aunt Jean"), who is still filling in gaps, and sometimes dropping bombshells!

My mom, Grandpa Jack, and Aunt Jean provided me with an overview of Grandma Sheila's parents and early life. Rae and Izzy, my great-grandparents, immigrated from Austria and Ukraine to New York City, where they met at a community-center dance on the Lower East Side and later got married. Sylvia (later, Sheila) was born in Manhattan in 1922. She was the third of four children: Sid was the oldest, next came Paula, then Sheila, and the youngest was Jean.

At the time I learned about my DNA, Aunt Jean was

approaching her nineties and still smart as a whip. She has always radiated positivity, with her happy smile, short blonde hair, and striking red lipstick. She nails the fashion game with her flowing slacks, stylish blouses, and well-coordinated nail polish. And she can still outpace me on a walk. Aunt Jean is the eldest connection in my maternal family history, and I treasure the close relationship we have.

After I received my DNA results, Aunt Jean had begun filling in some gaps. We spoke often on the phone, and still do. She's ninety-six now! During our conversations, I picture her in her fourth-floor apartment, sitting on her large L-shaped ivory sofa and looking out beyond the decorated garden just outside her glass balcony door. Even though she had some tough moments in the past, she is generally cheerful when she talks about our family. As I listen to her stories, I always take as many notes as I can.

In another one of our more recent phone conversations, which took place after I started writing this book, I asked Aunt Jean about her parents. Izzy, my great-grandfather, had been a tailor and operated his own cleaners. "He eventually worked seasonally for Ben Reig Designs, a high-end designer of clothing," she said. Rae (Rachel), my great-grandmother, had bright bluish-green eyes and was a beauty. Aunt Jean said, "She was a very smart woman and should have been born in *this* century. She was a very 'today' woman. She gave opportunities to lots of people without employment. She went into the lace business, and she used to go to lace manufacturers, collect large uncut rolls of lace, and give some out to other ladies to cut the patterns for wages. Once the pieces were cut, she would overlay them onto lingerie. Even if the women cut the pieces incorrectly, she still paid them and would fix the pattern. Your great-grandmother Rae was very generous and hardworking. She would have thrived in a more modern society." I thought how hard those times must have been for Rae, and how proud I was of my great-grandmother.

Rae passed away when I was five years old, and I still have faint memories of her. The first thing that comes to mind when I think of Rae is her beautiful mink coat, a gift from her third husband. Rae had been married three times. First to my great-grandfather Izzy, who passed away in 1961, then to Harry, who worked for an IBM store in Upstate New York. My Aunt Jean shared that Harry offered to buy Rae an extravagant diamond ring and she told him, "I don't need a diamond, I already have one! . . . You can buy me a mink coat." And so he did! I never got to meet Harry either, as he passed away before I was born and Rae remarried once again to a man named David. They lived in Florida until he became ill and was later checked into a home by his daughter. The mink from Harry went to Aunt Jean, but Rae would later acquire another mink that ended up in my grandmother's closet. And now, it's in my mother's closet. The three-quarter-sleeve mink coat has a mix of light and darker browns, and Rae's name is embroidered on the inside. The coat's length is just right for draping over an evening gown—it hits at the hip, so it doesn't steal the spotlight from your outfit. My mom wore the mink at my Roaring Twenties–themed birthday party when I turned forty years old. Maybe one day it will end up in my closet. It's fascinating how objects can make a full circle in a family—and what they can reveal, long after their original owners have passed.

Aunt Jean told me about her and Grandma Sheila's early years when their parents moved into the well-known low-income, nonprofit housing project called Lavanburg Homes on Goerck Street. Frederick L. Lavanburg donated a sum of money to get the project started in the Lower East Side. It is currently a six-story building with ninety-five apartments owned by the New York City Housing Authority. According to the *Jewish Daily*

Bulletin, Vol. IV (January 7, 1927), "About 120 families would be accommodated in four-room apartments renting at a rate of $6 a room per month."

Grandma Sheila was seven years old when Aunt Jean was born. Aunt Jean said, "I went to live with my grandmother until I was old enough to attend school because my parents had to work. My grandma would bring me home on the weekends to see the family, and by the time I was six, I moved back home with my sister Sheila and my parents. Sheila helped raise me. She was very good to me." Her voice wavered, and I could hear she was close to tears. "She was always very loving and very nurturing," she continued. "When I came home with head lice, Sheila would pick out all the nits from my hair and wash it!" Aunt Jean laughed.

She told me that Grandma Sheila was very adventurous and a little bit of a tomboy for her time. "If all the boys jumped in the East River, Sheila would jump in with them!" She said they both loved living at the Lavanburg homes. There were social centers in the basement of the building where adults and kids of all ages could get together and play games, watch movies, and do various activities. The Seniors' and Fathers' rooms offered cards, games, and billiards, while the Mothers' room offered books and cooking classes. Shoemaking was offered to the boys in the Juniors' room, and there were dollhouses, carriages, and seesaws in the Midgets' rooms. Each room would also screen films on certain nights of the week. This sounded like a great place for kids to grow up, I thought. No wonder Aunt Jean called it "the best place to live!"

During the summer months, Aunt Jean said there was a rooftop garden where they would plant flowers or vegetables and show movies starring Charlie Chaplin on an outdoor screen.

Before Aunt Jean and Grandma Sheila's brother Sid was drafted in the war, he used to rent a wagon to sell vegetables. Sid later fought in World War II, stepped on a landmine, and lost his leg. By the grace of God, he recovered and returned home to his wife and three children.

Even though both Rae and Izzy were working, Grandma Sheila had to quit school as a young teenager to work and help earn money, especially since there was a new child to take care of in the home. Growing up, I always sensed a mystery surrounding my "grandaunt," Barbara, who was called a "sibling" to Sid, Paula, Sheila, and Jean. Barbara was much younger than the others. My parents had cleared this up for me years ago when they told me that Barbara was not actually their sister but their niece (and my cousin)! Barbara was sixteen years old when she found out she was the biological daughter of Paula. She was born in 1936 when Aunt Paula was just eighteen years old. Although it was a hard decision, Aunt Paula agreed to allow her parents to adopt Barbara as their daughter. When Barbara was brought home from the hospital, they didn't have a crib for her, because, according to Aunt Jean, in the Jewish religion you weren't supposed to buy things for the baby before they were born. On Barbara's homecoming from the hospital, she slept in a dresser drawer for a few days until my great-grandmother and Aunt Paula purchased her crib.

It was not long after Barbara arrived that Grandma Sheila, in the eighth grade (according to census reports), dropped out of school, which according to Aunt Jean was very upsetting for Grandma Sheila. "She didn't want to leave school. She wanted to graduate with her class."

It was tough to earn wages in the 1930s, so she was instructed by her parents to follow her older sister Paula's footsteps, and as a young teenager, she went on the road to begin dancing. When Grandma Sheila first started out, Aunt Paula, a natural redhead, was working at the Gaiety Theater on Broadway in Manhattan (Minsky's), later becoming the Victoria

Theater and now the site of the New York Marriott Marquis Hotel.

That Grandma Sheila would be persuaded to join her older sister made sense considering my grandmother was already known for having a beautiful voice, great figure, and charisma. Multiple family members used to say what a shame it was that they couldn't have recorded her singing years ago. My mom remembers watching Grandma Sheila in the musical comedy *Guys and Dolls* at the Jewish center in Rosedale when my mom was about twelve years old. Grandma Sheila had the lead role as Miss Adelaide, and my mom said she was sensational, of course. Aunt Jean also told me how Grandma Sheila used to perform vocal numbers at their temple in Rosedale when they were younger and living next door to each other. "She was the star of their shows," she said.

I asked my aunt about when Grandma Sheila first got started in show business. The exact dates are unclear, but she had to lie about her age. When Grandma Sheila left school as a young teen, she started earning wages and would give the money to her parents, but one time, she took some of her earnings and bought Aunt Jean a Shirley Temple doll. Aunt Jean shared the story with laughter.

"Sheila gave me the doll and said, 'Don't tell Mom I gave it to you! If she asks, tell her you won it in a raffle.' I went along with it at first, but I was scared of telling a lie to our mother." Even though Rae eventually got the truth out of them, Aunt Jean was lucky enough to keep the doll.

It was after Grandma Sheila had been working for a few years that she met my Grandpa Jack at Coney Island. I asked Aunt Jean about this, relaying Grandpa Jack's version of that day at the pool, and she gave me hers. She laughed when I told her Grandpa Jack's story about their wedding and how they pulled people off the street.

Aunt Jean said that Grandma Sheila kept dancing off and on after marrying Grandpa Jack in 1947, but quit once and for all when my mother was young, becoming a homemaker and later a Girl Scout troop leader for my mom's troop. Grandma Sheila also worked in department stores off and on. Grandpa Jack and Grandma Sheila lived in their adorable three-bedroom home in Rosedale, Queens, next door to Aunt Jean and her husband, Eddie, in the early 1950s. According to Aunt Jean, Grandma Sheila was a wonderful mother who loved all of her children dearly and equally. She also shared how convenient and special it was to have her big sister next door for anything they needed.

When my mom was a teenager, the bank foreclosed on Grandpa Jack and Grandma Sheila's Rosedale home, so they returned to Los Angeles, where Grandma Sheila worked as a cosmetician in Studio City. I can imagine how sad Aunt Jean must have been to see them leave New York. Uncle Eddie and Grandpa Jack got along very well, their children were treasured playmates (despite the "terrorizing"), and Aunt Jean had become close to Grandpa Jack, too. She had a lot of respect for him. It's something I've grown increasingly aware of through our conversations: the fact that to this day she remains as intensely loyal to Grandpa Jack as to her sister.

Like Grandpa Jack, there were other, unexpected sides to Grandma Sheila. And not just her extensive dancing career. After doing my DNA, I learned that before she met Grandpa Jack, she had been married to an Italian waiter and bartender named Michael on her eighteenth birthday. He was a few years older than her and was drafted to the war shortly after their marriage. It was the 1940s, and Grandma Sheila's parents were very disapproving of the marriage because Michael was not Jewish—even though, according to Aunt Jean, Michael really loved Grandma Sheila and ended up converting to Judaism for her.

Aunt Jean recalled Michael, or Mike, as she called him,

bartending in Greenwich Village where Grandma Sheila took Aunt Jean after she graduated high school in 1946. "We went out for a drink after my graduation, and I vividly remember Mike behind the bar," she said. "I can still see him in my eyes, behind the bar shaking the shaker, making the drinks for us." Michael was still in the service, and when I talked about him with my mother, who'd never known about this earlier marriage, Aunt Jean concluded that he and Grandma Sheila must have divorced just before she met my grandfather in 1946. This means they would have been married for about six years in total. All fascinating facts, but no more than an incredible coincidence: it turned out this wasn't where the Italian came from because the years (and DNA) don't match up.

My sister and I were both honored to wear Grandma Sheila's diamond heart necklace on our wedding days, and I also borrowed something blue, which I held along with my bouquet—Grandma Sheila's white handkerchief with a blue embroidered letter S on it. I hope she enjoyed our string quartet's performance of one of her favorite pieces: the eighteenth variation of "Rhapsody on a Theme of Paganini, Op. 43." This piece is famously featured in various films, including *Somewhere in Time*, which was also one of Grandma Sheila's favorites, according to my mom.

My grandmother's story seems never-ending. Like the mink coat, I imagine her tale being passed down to my children, and how they might continue discovering and possibly unraveling our family's stories and weaving them with their own.

Even as I write this account, ongoing conversations with Aunt Jean continue to reveal more things I didn't know about my grandmother, and I wonder what I might find out next.

CHAPTER SEVEN: DANA

FEBRUARY 2018

On a sunny Friday afternoon, I was home alone, waiting. After I messaged Dana, James, and Maryann a few nights before, Dana had been the first of the cousins to reply, suggesting we chat over the phone on Friday afternoon. I wish I could have met her in person, but we were located on opposite sides of the country. She was in New Jersey, and I was in California. I was so restless. Since lunchtime, I'd been pacing my home office, picking up my phone in case I'd somehow missed her while checking the Ancestry site. I reread Maryann's message for the millionth time:

"I am looking for a first cousin (female), born in NYC around 1950."

Then in a moment, the phone rang and I answered. I was so nervous. Not just because I didn't know Dana, but suddenly I was afraid of what she might say. She sounded a little nervous, too. We were still complete strangers, even if we were related by blood. And in just a few minutes, I'd have a much better idea of how we were connected. But did I really want to know?

At first, I wasn't sure what to say. How do you start a conversation like this? I could tell we both wanted to rip the Band-Aid off, while at the same time, we didn't want to upset each other.

There was no instruction manual for this! What were the appropriate boundaries? How much should I ask about her personal life? How much should I tell her about mine? I'm sure we both had similar questions running through our minds, but Dana's voice was calm and kind as she began with the basics of who her parents were and gave me a quick family background. Our conversation went something like this:

"So, James is my father," Dana explained, "and Maryann is my father's first cousin. They have an uncle named Nino . . . so technically, my great-uncle." She said this with a little giggle, and I appreciated how she seemed to be trying to keep the tone light. Listening to Dana speak in a full New York accent gave me a strange sense of comfort. In a way, her voice immediately felt like home to me as it reminded me so much of my mother's side of the family.

"Okay," I said as I quickly jotted down these names and their connections.

Dana's dad = James; James & Maryann = 1st cousins; Nino = their uncle.

Then Dana gave me the main scoop: "So, what I found out was that Uncle Nino had a daughter in the 1950s for a while, and then she vanished. And basically, we were hoping that by doing our DNA, we might find her."

We were both silent for a moment. I went over her words in my mind. *Had a daughter for a while . . .* What does that mean?

Dana was very good about making sure I was comfortable and waited for me to give her the go-ahead before continuing.

"Alright, and . . . ?" I said.

"So no one ever knew what happened to the little girl, and no one ever questioned Nino, because apparently he didn't want to talk about it. When my cousin Maryann was a kid, she said she vaguely remembers her mother Nettie showing her a picture of a baby girl who was called 'Nino's daughter.'"

"Interesting," I said softly.

"It was Maryann who told my dad and the other cousins about Nino having a daughter. But no one ever knew the daughter's name. They just knew she existed."

The *daughter* . . . I replayed the words in my head. Though part of me was scared to hear more, I was in too deep now, and I kept quiet as Dana went on.

"The only thing my dad and Maryann knew for sure was that they definitely had a first cousin out there, but they had no idea if she was alive or dead, or what happened to her."

Whoa, this was deep, and so sad, I thought.

Dana continued, "The family thinks Nino's sister, Nettie, who is Maryann's mother, might have known more about his daughter back in the 1950s, but no one asked her questions when she was alive because all of my dad's cousins were so young at the time. Now everyone who might have known something is gone, and Nino also passed away in 2001 in Florida."

His daughter . . . The words kept repeating.

"But you know, now *anyone* can do a DNA test, so we were determined to find out what happened to that girl! Uncle Nino was really special to all of us . . . we absolutely loved him dearly, and that's why his daughter is also important to us," Dana said.

I was feeling a bit lost.

"Okay, can we back up? Who is Nino again?" I joked, doing my best to keep it together, though my head was starting to spin.

Dana laughed sympathetically.

"Sorry, I know it's a lot. So, Nino is my father's uncle, or in other words, my great-uncle or grand-uncle—however you want to say it," she laughed. "He has six siblings: Joe, John, Nettie, Grace, Frank, and Dewey. Nino is the sixth out of the seven siblings. Grace is my grandmother, and Nino's sister," Dana explained. I wrote down the names, repeating them back to her as I made my list.

"And where does Maryann fit?" I asked. "Who does she belong to?"

"Maryann is Nettie's daughter. So that makes her Nino's niece. Maryann is the one who thinks her mother Nettie may have known more about Nino's daughter because of the photograph Maryann remembers a long time ago."

I wrote down the connection between Maryann and Nettie:

Nettie = Maryann's mother, and Nino's sister.

"Okay, I just need a minute to process this. Can you tell me all the names again so I can make sure I wrote them down correctly?" I asked.

"Yeah, of course!" Dana took me through Nino's line again, naming each of his siblings one by one, and each of their children, too. I made a quick draft of their family tree. All six of Nino's siblings were married with children except for Nino. She confirmed: "He was never married, but he *did* have a child—he definitely had a daughter. We just don't know who she is or where she went, and that's what we are hoping to find out."

"This is so crazy," I said. "But it all makes sense now that I see who's who. Oh man . . . this is way more than I imagined I'd find out. I think I need some time to process all of this . . ."

Dana was very considerate and sensitive to the fact that she'd just given me a lot to digest. She was so patient and understanding.

I don't remember the rest of our call other than that we decided to pause the conversation for the time being so I could think things through and talk to my sister, too.

Before hanging up she said, "Call me anytime. I'm always here and happy to chat and answer any more questions. I'll check my photos and send you some of Nino so you can see what he looks like. I'll also send you a family tree with all the names so you can see everyone, as we figure this out."

"Oh, that would be great. Thank you so much," I said.

When we hung up, I began pacing again in my office. I was in shock and my mind was completely blown. I stared at the drafted family tree with the names Dana had given me:

*Joe — John — Nettie — Grace — Frank — **Nino** — Dewey*

Maryann	James	Mystery girl born in the 1950s

Dana

After my conversation with Dana, she texted me a few pictures of Nino. He was dressed very well, had a radiant smile, stood tall, had full dark hair and a sun-kissed complexion, and was quite attractive. I recalled my earlier conversation with Nathan and thought, if one of my grandparents wasn't my grandparent, and I was definitely, closely related to Nino's nieces and nephew, who were looking for a missing first cousin, "a girl born in the 1950s," could this actually mean...

Though I was still feeling nervous about everything I was thinking about, I called my sister only to discover yet another twist in the story! While I'd been processing Dana's revelation and looking at photographs, Rebecca had received a phone call from our uncle—mom's younger brother. He was very upset, telling Rebecca we needed to "stop all of this Ancestry stuff!" Then he proceeded to tell her a story about a time when Grandpa Jack had mentioned Grandma Sheila having an affair with an Italian man years ago.

As I listened, I thought: *Oh my gosh—could this be a confirmation?* But I let Rebecca finish.

"He told me apparently Grandma Sheila tried to run off with this man," she said, "but Grandpa Jack pulled a gun on him and told him to 'stay the hell away from his family!' And then he said Grandpa Jack didn't touch her for six months after that."

Even knowing what I knew, it was a shock to hear this.

"Was there any mention of the affair producing a child?" I asked.

"No, I didn't ask, but clearly the affair was known," Rebecca said.

I wondered, as did Rebecca, how he had known about our investigation of the Italian results. And why was he so upset? How was this *our* fault? I wasn't doing any digging without my parents' blessing: they'd both given me permission to investigate all aspects because they also wanted to know where the Italian came from!

Ancestry originally stated that based on our shared DNA, measured in centimorgans (cM), Rebecca and I had a predicted relationship with Dana, James, and Maryann as first or second cousins, so while listening to my sister, I had quickly written my shared centimorgans next to Maryann, James, and Dana and then plugged our names into the space underneath "Mystery girl born in the 1950s" on the drafted tree, just to see how it would fit:

Nettie	—	*Grace*	—	*Nino*	—	**(siblings)**
|		|		|		
Maryann (461cM)		*James* (529cM)		Mystery girl born in the 1950s		**(1C)**
		|		|		
		Dana (280cM)		**Me** **(or Rebecca)**		**(2C)**

My heart began to pound. *Oh my gosh—it works! We all fit perfectly together.*

Based on the shared centimorgans, I realized that my sister and I definitely fit Ancestry's suggested profile. Based on the numbers, we were unequivocally James and Maryann's first cousin once removed (1C1R) *and* second cousin (2C) to Dana.

One more confirmation, I thought.

It was time to tell Rebecca what Dana had said, and what I'd realized when piecing her information together.

I took a deep breath and exhaled, "So . . . I just plugged us into their tree to see how we fit. I can't believe this, but considering everything, it seems that Mom *could* be their missing cousin . . . which means, she *could* actually be Nino's missing daughter."

We were both quiet for a while, letting it sink in. I then explained the tree and the family lines with the centimorgans . . . more quiet . . . Rebecca knew as well as I did that there was no denying it. The evidence was beginning to pile up. "Nino could be our grandfather?" I said out loud for the first time, and the tears began to fall down my cheeks.

I could hear Rebecca's voice beginning to tremble as she said, "Oh my gosh, now what?" We sat for a few more moments in silence on the phone before hanging up. This was all insane.

Now what? That was the question I'd been asking myself ever since Dana's call. We would have to tell Mom what we found out —but when, and how? I wasn't ready to face this. Even with the DNA evidence, Dana's information, and our uncles' extra *twist*, my mind was still searching for another answer. The resurgence of denial and my refusal to accept a new truth emerged once again. You can't just undo a lifetime of believing in something. With my mom's DNA results yet to arrive, I held on to hope. And there was still some time left to gather more information. A couple days had passed by when I realized that I had another cousin to ask about my Syrian connection, and I would need to call her immediately.

CHAPTER EIGHT: JUDY

MARCH 2018

It was a lot to take in—the story from Dana, the angry phone call from our uncle, and the DNA results! I was still completely consumed with checking the Ancestry website, thinking the more I knew, the easier it would be to come to terms with things. But I wasn't quite ready to accept this new reality, and at the same time, my mind was still searching for ways out. That was when it dawned on me that there was one more piece that might prove I *was* Grandpa Jack's biological granddaughter: I had a Syrian cousin named Judy, who was closely related to Grandpa Jack—she was his niece! Her mother Frieda was Grandpa Jack's older sister. And, most significant, I remembered Bonnie mentioning that Judy had done a DNA test before me! Why hadn't I thought of this sooner?

So I went back to my DNA match list and carefully scrolled through the names . . . But Judy was nowhere to be found.

Oh no . . .

I called Bonnie first to ask if she knew anything about the Italians and whether or not Grandpa Jack could have been Italian. Her response: "There's no way!" Bonnie was married to Grandpa Jack's nephew, Mark and although Mark hadn't done his DNA, Bonnie was certain, based on all of her prior research of Grandpa Jack's family, that "Mark and Jack were Syrian through and through."

I had Judy's phone number and decided I needed to call her and double-check that she had, in fact, done a DNA test. If so, she could hold the key to our Syrian side.

But as anxious as I was to get on the phone with her, it would have to wait, at least until I'd finished a few urgent tasks. First, there was some Girl Scouts business to attend to. I was halfway through my first year of leading my daughter's troop, and our annual cookie sale was well underway. I still had to finish placing some last-minute online orders. I also needed to send out invitations for my sister's upcoming baby shower, and I also had a job interview for a teaching position scheduled for the following week, which I wanted to prepare for.

In between overanalyzing my DNA information, the effort to transition back to part-time work, and the responsibilities of family life—after-school sports, playdates, birthday parties, homework, cooking, laundry, and numerous other obligations—the mental checklist for that week seemed never-ending, and I could sense my blood pressure rising. But I still had a few hours of quiet that day before I needed to pick up my kids from school and begin my routine of running around. So, I decided to prepare and organize the invitations and cookie orders, and then contact Judy. The rest would have to wait.

I'd only met Judy in person a few times before, as she'd always lived on the East Coast, in New York and Pennsylvania. The last two times she visited California were for Rebecca's wedding in 2008 and to be at Grandpa Jack's home during his final days in 2013. Whenever I think back to the times I saw Judy, she had a welcoming presence around me, but most notable to me was how she and her Uncle Jack exchanged smiles, laughs, and hugs. It was very obvious to me that she absolutely loved him, and Grandpa

Jack clearly adored her. Even when she wasn't around, he spoke affectionately about her. I remember the photograph Grandpa Jack showed me when I interviewed him, of the two of them together when he was in the army. Aside from being close, they resembled each other in appearance.

At the time I called her, Judy was about seventy-eight years old. Our phone call happened something like this:

She answered in her New York accent, and I reminded her who I was: "Sharon, Michelle's daughter," I said. "Jack's granddaughter." I asked her how she was doing and explained that I was looking into something for the family and that I had a few questions. "If that's okay?" I asked.

"Hi, Sharon, yes, of course! Go ahead."

"Well, the first thing I wanted to know was whether or not you've ever done a DNA test?"

"Yes, a few months ago," Judy said. "I already got my results."

"Oh great! What company did you test with?"

"It was through Ancestry," she said.

My stomach dropped. But I persisted because I was still clinging to the hope that maybe, just maybe, somehow there'd been a glitch on my end. Despite my mounting distress, I tried to keep my voice calm . . .

"So, my sister and I did our DNA recently, and we both came back 25 percent Italian. Do you by any chance have any Italian?" *Please, please let this all just be a mix-up*, I begged silently.

"No way! I'm Middle Eastern. Our family is from Syria and Turkey," Judy said.

I inhaled deeply, then exhaled, trying to stop the heartache I felt creeping up from my stomach into my throat.

"Judy, can I ask you a favor? Can you log in to your Ancestry account right now and check if you see my sister, Rebecca, or me listed as your cousin? I don't see you on my side, and Rebecca doesn't see you either."

"You know, your grandfather is Syrian, too," Judy said. "You should be Syrian from your grandfather. Don't you see that on your side?"

"No, I don't . . . That's what I thought too, but there's no Syrian, no Turkey, no Arab whatsoever. It says we're 25 percent Italian and we are matched to three Italian cousins who are looking for a missing cousin. They have an uncle who had a daughter, and it's looking like that daughter could be my mom!" I said.

"No, no, no, *Jack* is your mother's father! He's not Italian, he's Syrian—I was there the day they brought your mother home from the hospital when she was born. Your grandfather was so happy." She spoke as if I was silly and mistaken. If only she was right. But unfortunately, it seemed that Judy, like me, was also in the dark. She had no idea about the Italian connection.

"Judy, I thought we were Syrian, too," I said. "But we don't have any Syrian in our DNA. We have Italian! Can you please check your Ancestry match list? I'm really hoping it's a mistake, but I need to be sure. If we are related through your Syrian side, we should be DNA-matched to you and should be on your match list." I explained this as best as I could while trying to stay calm.

"Well, you *should* be there. We're cousins!" Judy said. Clearly, she knew nothing about the Italians.

"I know, I thought so, too . . ."

"Okay, give me a minute and I'll get on my computer," Judy said, and I heard her moving around the room. I heard some tapping and clicking. "Right, I'm in . . . okay, DNA . . . DNA match list . . . I don't . . . no . . . I don't see your names at all here. Let me check again." She was quiet, and I could hear the sound of her mouse scrolling. I was checking mine, too, for what felt like the millionth time.

"I'm sorry, but I don't see you or your sister anywhere on my list." Judy sounded as bewildered as I felt, and my heart sank. If

Judy was my blood cousin from Grandpa Jack's Syrian side of the family, she would have to be on my DNA match list.

She wasn't.

It was confirmed: we were not biological cousins.

When we got off the phone, my head was in a whirlwind again and I felt completely crushed.

I sat for a few minutes staring at the screen, going over the call again, my head tight and aching in a way that was starting to feel familiar. Water, that's what I needed. I got up and went to the kitchen. I could hear the sound of the spring birds beginning to make their annual nest just above our kitchen window in the grapevines I'd planted years before. I didn't have to look up to know what they were doing. They returned to this spot every year. I poured myself a glass of water from the sink and blankly looked around my backyard through the window. My heart began beating fast as I held the cup, and I broke into tears.

We didn't have my mom's DNA results yet, but the evidence was piled up so high now, I'd started to accept the idea that this strange man, "Nino," might actually be my biological grandfather. Then, moments later, I reverted to complete denial all over again. What made all of this so much harder to deal with was the thought, which wouldn't leave me, that at some point my mother would find out. My cherished mother. I hated to think how this would affect her.

I took a breath and stared straight ahead at the four tall redwood trees just behind the swimming pool and thought, *What am I supposed to do now?* I wanted to run as fast as I could from all of it. I wanted to be one of those birds outside my kitchen window and fly away. I blamed myself for doing this stupid test to begin with: it was all my fault! I loved and adored my Grandpa Jack and my mother, and I hadn't intended for any of this to happen.

I walked back to my home office, picked up my phone, and

called Nathan at work. I was so upset, and pushing through tears and distress, I begged him to come home. When he arrived thirty minutes later, I completely fell apart in his arms. Nathan was so supportive and loving and reassured me that none of this was my fault—I couldn't possibly have known something like this would surface. Yet now my once-whole heart was completely shattered because *I* knew. Never mind if I didn't want to know it: the truth was staring me dead in the face.

Nathan held me tight and walked me to the sofa in our family room. We sat down together and I called my sister back, and with tears, I relayed my conversation with Judy. Rebecca logged in to Ancestry once more to check for Judy on her match list—but she wasn't there. We were both equally crushed and speechless. I held the phone in a semiconscious stupor for a few moments while Nathan sat quietly next to me, rubbing my back. Rebecca and I both took deep breaths, attempting to comprehend the elements of struggle within this revelation, as it was not a direct blow to us but rather a direct blow to our mother. Processing one's own heartbreak is one thing, which we were presently doing, but now I personally felt a sense of responsibility for what would become my mother's heartache, as I held this truth in my hands.

"I really hope Mom doesn't ask us about this," I said. "What are we going to do if she does? I mean, she's going to find out at some point!"

"She hasn't gotten her results yet," Rebecca said. "I think we should at least hold off until then."

"Right," I agreed. "And who knows, maybe something else will turn up . . ." I still couldn't shake my denial and hope.

Rebecca and I decided over the phone to try to keep the information to ourselves for as long as we could, while our mom's results were still pending.

And I began to pray.

CHAPTER NINE: QUESTIONS

MARCH 2018

People make hundreds of choices every day. What towel to wash their face with? What perfume or cologne to wear for the day? What to eat, what to wear, what to pack the kids for lunch? What route to drive to work or school? Some choices are so easy, we don't even think twice about them. But some choices are hard. They can affect the rest of your life. They can also affect the lives of those around you. And I had a colossal choice to make —whether or not to answer my mother's questions honestly, now that I had fully absorbed the scope of this entire situation. I tried to act as if it wasn't getting to me, but the burden of truth was suffocating.

I am a daughter who talks to my parents at least once a week, if not more. But since my conversation with Judy, I'd made a conscious decision to extend this as far as I could. To no avail: like clockwork, once a week had passed, the dreaded phone call came.

It was Mom.

We began with the usual back-and-forth. I asked her how she was, and then BOOM.

"So whatever happened with the Italians?" she said. "Did you ever get a response?"

My heart pounded, and in that split second, I had to make a decision. I couldn't lie to my mom! But also, I knew it would shatter every piece of her. The truth wouldn't just take the wind out of her sail; it would rip her sail in two. She was just calling to chat, not to find out that her father was *not* in fact her father, or at least not her biological father!

This was the choice I was faced with, and it came crashing down hard. *I should just be honest*, I thought. . . . Then, again: *How could I possibly do this to her?* My heart was already completely broken by what I *knew* would be revealed once her results came out. This was going to fracture her identity even more—just as it had mine. This was undeniably one of the most difficult decisions I would ever encounter in my life.

It was a huge dilemma, and it felt like a double-edged sword, as either choice carried consequences that weighed heavily on my mind. If I told her—I knew that outcome. If I said nothing, it would all unravel once her results arrived and she reached out to these people herself. They would tell her they'd talked to me, and then she'd have one more thing on her heart—that her own daughter had lied to her about something so monumental. That I hadn't warned her. That I hadn't been honest or done whatever it was I was supposed to have done. Ughhhh!!!

I wanted to scream. I wanted to run away. I wanted so many things, but not this! Please, Lord, not this! At that moment, my brain and my heart ran off in two different directions.

Then, suddenly it hit me.

Screw this! I was not going to carry this six-decade lie one step further. I would not lie, not even for my dearest grandparents. She *would* find out . . . and I was *not* the one who had done this to her. I was not the one who had lied all these years. The era of deception ends here! She was my mother and she deserved the truth. I would be a supportive daughter and we would get through this together. I swallowed the thick lump in my throat and replied.

"Um, yessss." I dragged my words as slowly as I could to buy myself a few more seconds. To spare her just a few more seconds of a life without heartbreak. "So, I did get a response, but it's heavy, very heavy..."

Then it struck me that there was another angle to this. There was another way I could look at the situation: Mom deserved the opportunity to *decide* if she wanted to hear the truth or not, and I felt obligated to give her this option. She was sixty-three-and-a-half years old and deserved to control her own reality. It wasn't much, but the thought gave me a small measure of comfort.

So I continued: "It's important you understand that if you *don't* want to know, we can bury the hatchet right now and I promise we will never talk about it again."

She responded simply and directly: "Spill it! Of course, I want to know!"

I said, "Mother, it's life-changing heavy. I don't know if you will want to know, to be honest. Maybe we should just wait until your results come back and then we can talk about it."

"Okay, you need to tell me!" she insisted.

Of course she wanted to know. But still, I persisted and asked her once more, "Are you sure you don't want to just think about it for a few days?" I paused briefly, then repeated, "Mother, it's life-changing... and it affects you, directly." I was praying in my mind she would say, "Okay, let me think about it." And that would be the end for the time being.

But again, she said, "I want to know!"

Anyone who knows my mom well knows that she doesn't like waiting for information. If she's watching a show, she's the person who will read spoiler alerts to find out what happens before the show airs. Which was also why I felt I at least had to give her a sense of the weight of what was coming.

I tried one last time. "You sure?"

She was.

"Okay, well, I think we should do a three-way call with Rebecca so we're all a part of this," I said.

"Why, why can't you just tell me?"

"Well, Rebecca has a piece of information, too, that she can share. It's just better that we all talk together. Let's get her on the line with us," I insisted. Calling one another over the phone to break this news wasn't ideal, but I lived over 350 miles away with two young children I couldn't leave home alone.

I closed my eyes, took another deep breath, and put Mom on hold while we got on a three-way call with my sister. Before I merged the call to include my mother, I quickly filled in Rebecca. I spoke as fast as I could, feeling like a sped-up record played in a chipmunk's voice as I explained that Mother wanted to know about the Italians and that I'd tried to dissuade her from investigating further, but I couldn't lie.

"I told her we should wait till she gets her results back, just to be 100 percent certain, but she wants to know now! Dammit! She's on the other line, and I thought we should do a three-way call so we're all involved . . ."

"Oh boy . . . Okay," Rebecca said. "Well I guess we need to tell her sooner rather than later . . . she's going to find out anyway."

"Yeah, those are my thoughts, too. Ugh! Okay, I'm going to merge her in now . . . Hang on," I said.

Another deep breath.

The calls merged.

"Hello . . . hey." Rebecca's voice was casual and cheerful.

But by this point, my mom was suspicious and somewhat irritated.

"So what's going on, you guys?" she said.

After explaining the scenario to Rebecca, as if I hadn't already clued her in, I began: "Okay, so, you guys know that I wrote to Dana, James, and Maryann—the three cousins from my DNA match list—like we talked about," I reminded her.

"Yeah . . . ?" my mom interrupted.

"Just so you have the context, I'll read you the message I sent to all three of them," I said.

"Looks like you came up as a DNA match on my account. Wondering how? I didn't even know that I was Italian. Who were your grandparents and great-grandparents and where were they from?"

Mom and Rebecca were silent.

"So that was my message," I said, "and this was their response." I read them the reply I'd received from Maryann three days later.

"I am looking for a first cousin (female) . . . born in NYC around 1950. So it may be your Mom or Grandma. How do we contact one another?"

The phone was still silent. I said, "Are you guys still there?" They both said, "Yes."

"So after I read the message from Maryann, I contacted both her and Dana and gave them my phone number, and Dana was the first to respond," I explained.

"So, wait, do they think I'm their cousin? I was born in 1954," Mom said.

I hesitated. "Yes, they think you might be. But let me just tell you the story that Dana gave me when she called."

I explained what Dana had said about her Uncle Nino having a daughter who was born in New York in the 1950s and then vanishing suddenly, and how no one had ever gotten to meet her and didn't even know her name or whether she was alive or dead.

"Everyone wondered what happened to the little girl who was their missing cousin," I said.

Silence.

"Mother, it's more than likely it's *you* they're talking about."

The phone remained silent.

Then Mom said, "Wait, what are you talking about?! How can I be their missing cousin?"

"I know. That's what's been going through our minds, too!" I said. I repeated the message from Dana. "Her uncle had a daughter around the time you were born. And like you said, you were born in 1954. This is also why Rebecca needs to be on this call . . . she has something to share with you, too, from your brother," I said.

Rebecca then told Mom what our uncle had said about a time when Grandma Sheila was having an affair with an Italian man a long time ago.

"Grandpa apparently met them at a courthouse where Grandma was going to run off and possibly try to marry this other man, but Grandpa went there and told her to get her ass home, then apparently pulled out a gun and threatened the man! Grandpa told the Italian man to stay away from his family."

There was silence on the phone, longer this time.

"Mother, we need to see what your DNA shows to be 100 percent certain, but Rebecca and I have no traces of Syrian. Only Italian. On the one hand, the Italians have their story, and on the other hand, we have this story from your brother . . . and then we have the DNA in the middle of it all," I said.

Still silent.

"So wait . . ." Mom said. "These people have been looking for me?"

"Apparently?" I said in a questioning tone.

"Apparently, yes," Rebecca confirmed.

I continued, "But, Mother . . . there's also one more detail I just found out . . ." I knew this was going to be the bombshell, and I braced myself . . .

"Cousin Judy also did her DNA a few months ago on Ancestry" —deep breath— "She's *not* on our DNA match list as a cousin . . . or *any* kind of relative. I spoke to her on the phone, and she confirmed her results were from Syrian and Turkish regions. She has no Italian whatsoever. She said Grandpa and her side were Syrian through and through. I thought Ancestry had made a mistake, so I asked her to check her DNA match list. She did. Rebecca and I are *not* on her match list either."

The final blow . . .

"This means we're not blood-related to the Syrian family—like, at all. We have no Syrian," I repeated. "And Judy has no Italian. Of course, we need your DNA results to 100 percent confirm it, but all of this *strongly* suggests . . . that Grandpa is not your biological father."

And that was it. Her world completely collapsed.

Her sail, torn into two.

A sudden, jarring clunk resonated in my ears. It was the sound of my Mom's phone hitting the ground, and we could hear her yelling and crying, "No, no, no, this can't be!" My dad picked up the phone. "Your mother is crying," he said in tears. My sister and I were in tears, too. Jack was our grandpa! He was our world. Rebecca and I did not want this to be true any more than our mom did! Bonnie and I had shared research about Jack's whole family. I knew all the names of the Syrian family—*my* family! I was Syrian, too! How could this be happening? It was absolutely devastating. And now, my mother's heart was left in ruins. Why did this ever have to fall into my lap? What had I done?

My mom came back to the phone. Her voice was shaky and upset, but she had her own questions about Nino.

"What was their uncle's name again?"

"Nino . . . Nino Napolitano," I said.

"Is this guy still alive?" she asked.

"No, he died in 2001," I said through tears and gave her the whole story based on what Dana shared with me about Nino's background.

"Mother, I'm so sorry. We never wanted to hurt you," I said.

"I don't blame you guys. You asked me if I wanted to know... Of course, you didn't mean to hurt me, I know that," Mom said. "I know I'll have many questions, but I need time to process this. I think I need to make some phone calls."

"Of course," Rebecca and I answered in unison.

"Your results will be official confirmation," I reminded her, still holding on to some hope this was all a misunderstanding, even though I truly knew it wasn't.

We got off the phone shortly after that. I sat slumped in my office chair for a few minutes until I pulled myself up to look at the pictures Dana had sent me of Nino on the phone one more time. In the hallway, I could hear the faint sounds of my kids giggling in their rooms and noticed it was already dark outside. Nathan was in the living room sitting on the couch in the dim light. One of Nathan's (many) exceptional traits is his ability to read a room and understand when there are no adequate words for a given situation. He immediately got up, walked over to me, and grabbed me, without uttering a single word. He knew exactly what to do as he just held me tight and I sobbed in his arms.

This phone call was by far the hardest thing I'd ever been faced with in my entire life. To tell my own mother that her father wasn't her father.

Frustration, regret, and deep sorrow were all I felt.

Then a fire lit under me, and I became angry and determined. The gloves were off, and I wanted to know everything. Nothing was going to stop me from getting as much truth and information as I could. Not just for me, but for my mom. I had a million questions, and I know she did, too, and sixty-three years had been long enough! Finding answers was the least I could do at this point. Guilt hung over me, and all I wanted to do was give my mother some peace. And I had another idea: there was one more person I could talk to. Aunt Jean was still alive. Surely, she would have something to tell me. I decided I needed to call her right away.

CHAPTER TEN: JEAN

MARCH 2018

After breaking the news about Nino to my mother and witnessing her heartbreak, I was anxious to help her. I wanted to find answers to her many questions, but there weren't many people left to ask, with Aunt Paula and Barbara having passed away just a few years before I got my DNA results. I looked back at my conversations with Grandpa Jack, Bonnie, Judy, and even "Cookie," as well as the interview, wishing I'd known what questions to ask back then. There was really only one person who might be able to help, and that was my Aunt Jean, Grandma Sheila's youngest sister. She was my last connection to the family history, the last person from Grandma Sheila's generation who might have some insight, and my only real hope for any information about this stranger, Nino. She was surely also the best person to ask given her closeness to Grandma Sheila and the fact that they'd lived right next door to each other in the 1950s when my mother was born!

In all my many wonderful conversations with Aunt Jean, one theme that would come up time and time again was how good Grandma Sheila was to Aunt Jean growing up.

Jean and Sheila

"She was the *best* big sister," Aunt Jean would say. It always made my heart so happy to hear the affection in her voice and to sense the love she held for her older sister decades after losing her. I feel the same about Aunt Jean, as does Mom. She has always been a beloved aunt to my mother, sister, and me. In so many ways, she reminds us of Grandma Sheila, whom we adored and lost so early. It's tough to go through life missing someone you care about so much, and Aunt Jean has faced losses that are too painful to imagine. She's a true warrior.

Still, it was a hard call to make. How would Aunt Jean react? It hadn't been easy telling Mom, and part of me wished I didn't have to be the one to bring up this topic again, this time with my aunt. With Aunt Jean already approaching her nineties, I could understand there might be things she would rather leave in the past. But I had to do it, for Mom. So before the call, I went through all the genealogy records I had gathered to date, including the information Dana had given me, keeping an eye out for anything I might have missed around the time Mom was born.

In all my conversations with Aunt Jean, I never got tired of hearing her talk about her and Grandma Sheila's childhood growing up on the Lower East Side, in a neighborhood that Aunt Jean said was widely known as one of the most historic neighborhoods in America, and which was home to many European immigrants and the working class who lived in the crowded, tall, and narrow tenements. She mentioned laundry flapping in the wind, hanging from balconies, fire escapes, or the long clothing lines stretching from one building to the next and how there was no room for gardens, trees, or lawns. When I read Hasia R. Diner's book *Lower East Side Memories*, I learned that the Lower East Side was "especially remembered as a place of Jewish beginnings for Ashkenazi American Jewish culture." And my family was a big part of that, having lived through European oppression, most of them escaping the Holocaust and immigrating to the U.S., where they found freedom and the opportunity to thrive and rebuild the Jewish community they'd left behind.

It was fascinating to hear what it was like when Aunt Jean lived there, nearly a century ago, and I could tell how much she enjoyed talking about it, frequently repeating how she'd loved growing up there. She told me how she and their family would go shopping on Orchard Street, where vendors would set up booths and sell merchandise and foods like meat, eggs, potatoes, and seasonal produce, which were popular in the very crowded booths. You would often hear people yelling in Yiddish, trying to negotiate fair prices. There were pushcart vendors on Rivington Street, and it was a real treat to get a sugar-coated jelly apple on a stick or a Charlotte Russe cake for a treat on certain days, she told me. The Charlotte Russe cake came in a small, ruffled cardboard holder full of layered whipped cream and yellow cake.

Many of the peddlers also sold different assortments of nuts or candies on their pushcarts, which sat parked along the curb in the street.

Aunt Jean was a keen swimmer, and in summers she went as often as she could to the Hamilton Fish Park, where it cost a quarter to swim all day from 10 a.m. to 5 p.m. My great-grandmother Rae would bring Aunt Jean lunch at the back gate of the swimming pool, where she spent the whole day.

By the time Aunt Jean was a teenager, Aunt Paula and Grandma Sheila were earning money on the road as full-time dancers. Aunt Jean spent her adolescent years in school and helping her parents take care of her little "sister" Barbara (Aunt Paula's biological daughter).

"One time Barbara got her head stuck in a gate," Aunt Jean said, "and I had to run and get Mr. Schaeffer, the Lavanburg building supervisor, to help me get her out. I was like a mother to her. She was my responsibility during the day. I always looked after her, and she loved to tag along with me and my friends."

It sounded like Aunt Jean was as great of an older sister to Barbara as Grandma Sheila was to Aunt Jean. And Aunt Jean could be similarly strong-willed and single-minded, too, as I was reminded when she told me about the day she first met Grandpa Jack when she was about seventeen years old. Despite Grandma Sheila and Grandpa Jack's attempt to set Aunt Jean up with one of Grandpa Jack's friends the day they all met at Coney Island, Aunt Jean said she wasn't interested. She already had her sights on a man she adored . . . her future husband, Eddie.

Uncle Eddie was drafted by the U.S. Navy at eighteen years old, and she met him while he was still in the service. They were a part of the same group of friends that attended the same social clubs. The only snag was that Uncle Eddie didn't want a girlfriend at the time, because he wanted to finish college first. So Aunt Jean decided to go out with someone else, but when Uncle

Eddie heard whom she was seeing, he told her, "That guy's no good for you." They began to date shortly after that. They dated for about a year and a half, and two weeks after Uncle Eddie's college graduation, they got married at the Manhattan Center in New York on February 19, 1949. Grandma Sheila had been married to Grandpa Jack for two years by this time. Aunt Jean and Uncle Eddie's wedding cost a total of $2,000 for two hundred people. They honeymooned at the Laurel in the Pines Hotel in Lakewood, New Jersey, so they could see a popular comedian who was performing at that time.

In the early 1950s, Aunt Jean started working as an interior designer, a career she entered because of the confidence Grandma Sheila gave her.

"Sheila recommended that I go into interior design because she thought I had a knack for it," Aunt Jean said. "So I went to school for it." Grandma Sheila was right: Aunt Jean has a strong eye for design and has decorated many family members' homes. She kept working until she and Uncle Eddie had their first child, Debbie, in 1952. It was during this time that they lived in Rosedale, Queens, right next door to Grandma Sheila, Grandpa Jack, and their nearly one-year-old son, Steven (Mom's older brother). Two years later, in 1954, Grandma Sheila gave birth to my mother, and the following year, in 1955, Aunt Jean and Uncle Eddie had their second daughter.

The four cousins grew very close, even though my mother became a known "terror" to her cousins over the years. According to Aunt Jean, Mom would "wash" the girls' hair with sand and pretend it was shampoo! She laughed when she told me this.

When Debbie was very young, Aunt Jean used to bring her to the beach at a place called the Sound View Hotel in Milford, Connecticut, to play with her cousin Steven. Aunt Jean would watch the two kids while Grandma Sheila worked inside the hotel.

Then, a few years later, tragedy struck, and Debbie became deathly ill with cancer. I'll always remember Aunt Jean's words, the first time she spoke to me about this.

"Debbie told me that she wanted a baby brother, and I felt that in Debbie's own way, she was giving me permission to go on with my life. So I became pregnant with my third child in Debbie's last year of life."

I could see how hard it was for Aunt Jean to talk about Debbie, and her pain touched me deeply, but Debbie is a special part of our family, and I wanted her to be known in this story.

Sadly, Debbie never got to meet her youngest baby sister, as she passed away about six weeks before she was born in 1960. Debbie was only seven years old, and through all the tears and heartache, Aunt Jean told me it was Grandma Sheila who got her through the death of Debbie.

In my opinion, Debbie is a spitting image of her first sister. They're both tall and have beautiful, flowing, dark hair. In older pictures, I have a hard time telling them apart. The baby, in contrast, is a blonde beauty, like Aunt Jean. I wish I could have known Debbie. All three of her daughters are beautiful girls.

Uncle Eddie and Grandpa Jack got along very well, and over the years, they formed a strong bond. Aunt Jean and Uncle Eddie took many trips with their children, but in the late 1960s, they decided to take a trip to Israel with Grandpa Jack and Grandma Sheila while Aunt Jean's girls were away at summer camp. My mom and her brothers were old enough to be home alone at that time. While in Israel, Grandpa Jack was able to speak in Arabic to the locals and ask for directions or questions. He also understood the crude remarks that two men were making about Grandma Sheila and Aunt Jean, as Aunt Jean told me, "Jack being Jack, he stood up for us and yelled at them in Arabic ... It was very impressive." I could tell the trip had been a happy and memorable one, as Aunt Jean still remembered it in detail, like the evening she went to dinner with only Grandpa Jack because Grandma Sheila and Uncle Eddie got food poisoning. I always saw Aunt Jean and Grandpa Jack's friendship as a devoted one, as they were very close and enjoyed each other's company. On another night, the four of them went out dancing and Grandma Sheila went onstage and put on a show for the crowd.

"Your grandmother was born to entertain," Aunt Jean said, repeating what I'd heard often about Grandma Sheila's beautiful voice and outgoing personality.

In 1999, on the Las Vegas road trip I went on with Grandpa Jack, before my first recorded interview with him, Aunt Jean and Uncle Eddie were there, too. We drove from LA in Grandpa Jack's white Toyota Cressida and stayed at the Tropicana Hotel, his favorite regular spot, where he had made numerous "connections" over the years he visited. While the men gambled, Aunt Jean and I walked through almost every lobby of the largest hotels on the strip because she was determined to see the inside of each one. She was three times my age and completely wore me out physically. I couldn't keep up with her. We ate at buffets, and it was the first time I'd ever seen escargot on a menu. Of course, that's what she ordered, and she tried to get me to taste one, but there was absolutely no way I would. At that time in my life, I was nowhere near brave enough to branch out and sample such a delicacy. I was still a kid. She was sweet and didn't push me.

Sadly, the Tropicana Hotel is no longer part of the Las Vegas Strip. I watched it crumble to the ground on television in 2024. A part of my heart felt very sad to see it demolished, but I'm grateful for the memories I made there with Aunt Jean, Uncle Eddie, and Grandpa Jack on that trip.

In 1991, following Grandma Sheila's death, our whole family flew out to New York to visit some of our relatives, including

Aunt Jean and Uncle Eddie, who were living in Secaucus, New Jersey, at the time. Grandpa Jack took us to my mother's childhood home in Rosedale, Queens, where she and her siblings and cousins shared some of their fondest childhood memories before she and Grandpa Jack moved to California. I was also able to see the home where Aunt Jean had lived next door.

Grandpa Jack and Grandma Sheila's home was a white two-story with a small patch of grass and a brick walkway leading up to the porch. There was one small tree in the front yard with a brick border that encircled it at the base. Aunt Jean and Uncle Eddie's home next door had a similar style but was painted differently. My mom showed us the fire alarm on the corner that she'd pulled as a prank when she was a child. I can't believe the fire alarm was still there after all those years. Now, looking back, I also can't believe my mother lived so close to Nino, who resided in the Bronx!

In 1999, Aunt Jean and Uncle Eddie celebrated their fiftieth wedding anniversary in Florida, and we attended as a family—my mother, father, sister, and me. I remember Aunt Jean saying in the most upbeat and happy tone, "The best years of my life were after retirement! No more worrying about kids, college, and everything else. At seventy years old, we were at the peak of our lives!! And we were still on our honeymoon!" Then she added, "You know you can still have a honeymoon at seventy, right?!" I was always so inspired and warmed by Aunt Jean and Uncle Eddie's love for each other.

At the time of the anniversary party, Nino was living in Florida just minutes away from where the party was located. Looking back on that trip, I really wish we could have knocked on his door if we had known what we know today. The idea that I was physically close to his home hits even harder knowing that Nino passed away just two years after that party.

Aunt Jean's smile, love, energy, and enthusiasm were contagious, and Uncle Eddie was always so sweet—and he was a crack-up, too. One afternoon during that trip to Florida we were driving in a separate car following Uncle Eddie to a location I can't recall. He turned around ahead of us and the next thing I remember was seeing Uncle Eddie driving on the wrong side of the street! It was a busy road with many cars, and my dad and Grandpa Jack yelled, "Wrong way, Eddie!" (As if he could hear them.) I remember him just carrying along with his usual smile on his face, clueless as to what everyone was yelling about. To this day, we refer to Uncle Eddie as "Wrong-Way Eddie."

Uncle Eddie was just as beloved to us as Aunt Jean, and being so close to Grandpa Jack, I wished he was still around. Aunt Jean and Uncle Eddie's eldest daughter told me that before her father passed away in 2015, he had shared with her how Grandpa Jack had come to him in a dream. He said they were in a bar laughing it up, and Grandpa Jack was smiling like always. It had seemed so real, Uncle Eddie told her. Shortly after that dream, Uncle Eddie passed away, and we like to think that maybe Grandpa Jack was there to take him home.

All these memories were playing through my mind the day I'd planned to call Aunt Jean. It was a sunny day in the middle of March 2018. I had just come home from picking my kids up from elementary school. My daughter was in first grade and my son was in third grade at the time. They had just been running through a grassy green hill filled with mustard-seed flowers and looked so cute covered in yellow pollen. I got them cleaned up and settled with a snack, then told them I'd be on a phone call for a little bit so they should stay quiet in their rooms until I was finished. I had my notes in front of me, and despite my nerves, I was feeling hopeful that Aunt Jean would have the answers my mom needed.

After a few rings, Aunt Jean answered on her landline. I asked her how she was, and she asked about the kids.

"Everybody okay?" Aunt Jean said. Not much got past her, and it seemed that she had quickly picked up on my anxiety. Aunt Jean loves my children, always telling me how beautiful they are and to send them her love. They've seen her multiple times over the years, and these meetings are always precious. She gives them treats like cookies or little candies and showers them in hugs.

"Oh, yes, they're doing well. We're all okay . . ." I took a deep breath. There was no point pretending I had called her just to chat when we both knew this wasn't true.

We continued our conversation very close to the following:

"Aunt Jean, I'm calling because I have to ask you something very important," I said.

"Okay . . ."

"Rebecca and I did our DNA recently, and it came back 25 percent Italian. I have no idea why, and I'm hoping you can help." I spoke fast, wanting to get all the facts out before I lost my nerve.

"We've been matched to three Italian cousins. One cousin wrote to me that they're searching for their first cousin. Another one told me a story about their uncle who had a daughter and they don't know what happened to her. I just have to ask you . . . is there any chance the name Nino Napolitano rings any bells?"

Aunt Jean paused briefly, then said, "No, I don't know of anyone by that name."

"Do you remember Grandma Sheila having an affair while you guys were neighbors in Rosedale? Was there ever anything suspicious going on at home that you can think of?"

She answered, "No, I didn't know of anything going on." Trying not to feel disappointed, I continued.

"Do you know if anyone else in the family knows anything? Did Grandpa Jack know that Mom wasn't his biological daughter?" I kept my tone gentle, not wanting to upset Aunt Jean, but I was starting to feel desperate. I had so much information already. I just needed to fill in the blanks—surely she must know something, I thought.

"Mom also knows everything I know," I added. "She asked me about my results, and I couldn't lie to her . . . Plus, she also took her DNA test, so she's going to get her results any day now. We're just trying to make sense of all this. We all thought we were Syrian, but there's only Italian. If you know anything extra, it would be really helpful."

Aunt Jean responded, "Okay, I will . . . I'm very sorry. I wish I could tell you more, but I really don't know anything about it."

I could imagine she must be feeling quite shocked and confronted so suddenly with all this information. It was a lot to process. Then, just when I thought she wasn't going to say anymore, she started talking again.

"I do remember one time, there was something . . ." she said. "It was the night I went into labor. . . . We got up at two in the morning, and Ed went to take Debbie next door to Sheila's before we left for the hospital. When Ed came back, he said he heard a noise like a shuffle in the background as Sheila met him at the door. He said it sounded like a man's pair of shoes fell on the floor and that maybe someone was hiding. We thought it was strange because Jack wasn't home that night, but we didn't ask questions because I was busy having a baby!"

I had a lot of questions about this. But I sensed not to push her anymore today, that it would be counterproductive, and I didn't want to cause her any distress. At least this was a start, and maybe, if I waited, she might remember more. It was a very conflicting moment for me. I deeply respected and loved Aunt Jean way too much to harass her for more information, and the last thing I wanted was to undo a sacred bond between two sisters, if she did know more. I so much admired Aunt Jean's love and loyalty to her cherished sister, but I was also desperately hoping to hear more, especially since they were next-door neighbors during that entire time!

I said goodbye and asked Aunt Jean to let me know if she thought of anything else. She said she would. And though it would be years before more details were discovered, she kept her word.

CHAPTER ELEVEN: RESULTS

MARCH 26, 2018

It was now March 26, a date I'll never forget for a number of reasons. First, it was Grandma Sheila's birthday—she would have been ninety-five years old in 2018. Second, March 26 was the day she married her first husband, Michael, at the age of eighteen. But most significantly, March 26 was the day my mom found out she was Italian.

Her DNA results were as follows: 49 percent Southern Italy, 51 percent Ashkenazi Jewish. And . . . nothing else. ZERO percent Syrian.

She also carried the appropriate amount of centimorgans to place her as a direct first cousin to James and Maryann and first cousin once removed (1C1R) to Dana, James's daughter.

My father's DNA carried the remaining German, British, Baltic, and French traits. He was 0 percent Italian, just as Grandma Lorraine had said. Grandma Lorraine was my last living grandparent at the time, and her DNA had also come back matching the traits of my father (thank goodness!).

I had been speaking to Dana frequently over the phone, and we'd discussed starting a group chat to include the other Italian cousins, along with my mom and sister, so we could exchange information and pictures. I was determined to gather as much information as I could to figure out more about this story.

The group chat began on March 26—the same day my mother got her results—and the warm welcome messages started to pour in from all of our newest cousins, followed by pictures, stories, and contact information. They wanted to help as much as possible in figuring out more details, and several of Nino's nieces and nephews ended up taking a DNA test. My mom would later be matched to ALL of them as first cousins (1C), leaving only one option left...

It was official: Grandpa Jack was *not* my mom's biological father. And he was *not* my biological grandfather. Nino was.

Reflecting on all my conversations and the interview with Grandpa Jack, there was still one distressing question that I wish I could have asked him during our interview if only I'd had this information then: "Did you know Mom wasn't your biological daughter?"

Whether he knew or not, one thing was certain: Grandpa Jack loved and raised my mother, and *nothing* could ever change this fact. Still, the question as to whether or not he'd known remained a source of distress for my mom, and we were determined to seek the whole truth.

CHAPTER TWELVE: COUSINS

APRIL 2018

After getting her DNA results, my mom began making phone calls to her cousins on her maternal side of the family. As it turned out, Grandma Sheila's affair hadn't been much of a secret. In fact, every single one of Mom's maternal first cousins knew about the affair, as well as the fact that my mom wasn't Grandma Jack's biological daughter! As the phone calls carried on, so did the multiple stories, and they were all happy to share what they knew.

Cousin Bernice was about twelve when she began babysitting Mom's older brother Steven, while Grandma Sheila was pregnant with my mom. Bernice had a strong memory of seeing two Italian brothers. She couldn't forget them if she tried, she said, because they were so handsome, especially Nino. Bernice said they used to all play on the beach and go clam-digging together. During the conversation, she also mentioned a place called the Emerald Room, where she said Grandma Sheila was working at the time. *The Emerald Room??*

Though Mom knew her mother had performed in musicals, she didn't know much about where she'd performed and had never heard of the Emerald Room until this conversation. She wrote down all of the information Bernice had given her and shared it with me.

Next, she spoke to our cousin Al, Barbara's ex-husband. Al said he used to drive a taxi and had often driven Grandma Sheila to and from the Emerald Room at the Sound View Hotel in Milford, Connecticut! He said Grandma Sheila had danced there for a few years. Occasionally, she would stay overnight and tell Al she didn't need him to drive her home. Al said he never saw Nino, but he always wondered why Grandma Sheila would stay the night. Later, he *heard the talk* at the family gatherings about Grandma Sheila's affair but never asked questions because he didn't feel it was his place. That seemed to be a shared feeling among all of Mom's cousins.

The phone calls continued, and multiple cousins said they'd overheard their parents or other cousins talking about Grandma Sheila, Nino, and the baby. They all said the same thing—they'd known of my grandmother's relationship, but it wasn't their place to speak about it, and certainly not their place to ask questions. Though part of me shared my mom's frustration and disappointment that no one had ever said anything, I had to accept that times were very different then. And I was learning how it felt to be "the messenger" with my mom. Still, I couldn't stop thinking about how they'd all known all along, and for so many years, that Grandma Sheila had a baby with another man. But what if Mom hadn't been kept in the dark? If she'd known, how would her life have been different? Would she have found Nino, and how might this have changed the course of things? The possibilities were endless as I considered these "parallel lives." Would Rebecca and I even be here if Mom had discovered the truth sooner and possibly stayed in New York instead of moving to California, where she met my dad after Grandpa Jack lost their home in Rosedale?

While it was clear that we had been kept in the dark about

Grandma Sheila having a baby with another man, there was one thing everyone was unsure about: no one could say for certain whether or not Grandpa Jack knew the truth. This was the question burning in our minds.

Then my mom called her older brother Steven. He was about four or five years old at the time when Grandma Sheila worked in Milford and was regularly babysat by Bernice. He said he didn't remember much being so young and had no idea about the affair *or* that she wasn't Grandpa Jack's biological daughter!

Once she'd spoken to her maternal side, Mom started contacting the cousins on Grandpa Jack's side of the family. But first, she began with a dear friend of Grandpa Jack's, Irving, to see if he knew anything. He said no and was completely shocked to hear her story! The phone calls followed with Bonnie (the Syrian genealogy expert) and her husband Mark, who was Grandpa Jack's nephew. She also spoke to Judy, Grandpa Jack's niece, whom I'd previously spoken to. Strangely, no one on Grandpa Jack's side seemed to know anything about the affair or whether or not Grandpa Jack was Mom's biological father. So it wasn't just us in the dark. We thought it was very interesting that Grandpa Jack's family and Irving were in the dark, too. Could it be that he never knew? Or had he known and just kept it to himself?

After gathering stories and information from each cousin, this was now the most troublesome question: Did Grandpa Jack know that my mom wasn't his biological daughter? I thought, surely someone's gotta know something!

CHAPTER THIRTEEN: BURLESQUE

In addition to my quest to find out what Grandpa Jack knew, I was also very intrigued about the place Bernice had mentioned: the Emerald Room. I was hopeful that I would uncover something significant. A quick search revealed that it wasn't just a venue for musicals and theater, but was known for a different kind of entertainment . . .

I began a newspaper subscription to dig into the archives. To my surprise, I discovered multiple advertisements spanning a two-year period from December 1954 to December 1956 starring "Sheila Lind" at the Emerald Room in the Sound View Hotel, in Milford, Connecticut.

Based on these dates, my mother was about four months old when Grandma Sheila must have returned to work there. Each advertisement presented the same blurry black-and-white photo of Grandma Sheila smiling in a sexy pose, in heels, one toe pointed, and wearing a two-piece outfit: a short skirt with a long train down the back and a bralette top. Her left hand was on her hip, and her right hand touched the side of her head, which was tilted back seductively. I was blown away and reminded of the "weird" painting above Grandpa Jack's bed that looked like her:

the dark-haired, naked woman in a sexy pose, with the piece of fabric that resembled a snake.

All of these advertisements validated Bernice's, Al's, and Aunt Jean's claims that Grandma Sheila had worked at the Sound View Hotel's Emerald Room, and also confirmed the time frame when Bernice babysat Steven and met the two Italian brothers on the beach in the summer months.

In addition to the Emerald Room advertisements, I found several more dating back to the 1940s. One that caught my eye was an article describing Sheila Lind doing "a striptease in a red gown and red light, calling forth whistles and exclamations from the audience."

A striptease! I'd known about the singing and dancing, and I'd seen showy photos of her, but stripping? I should have been used to the unexpected when it came to my grandmother by now, but this still shocked me.

I thought of the eight-by-ten-inch black-and-white photo Grandpa Jack had shown me years ago of Grandma Sheila in her polka dot dress, legs kicked up in the air. Grandpa Jack had actually given the original to me, and it has hung on my wall to this day. But in all the hundreds of times I looked at it over the years, it never crossed my mind that in addition to performing in musicals as a singer throughout the 1940s and 1950s, Grandma Sheila was a stripteaser. It finally sank in for me! That's what she'd done when she left school and went "on the road" with my Aunt Paula as a teenager. She was a rising burlesque dancer! I felt so naive.

Going by these advertisements, Grandma Sheila had performed across the United States, from Los Angeles to Milford. I also found many advertisements of Aunt Paula, whom I'd learned went by the stage name Rusty Lane, at the famous burlesque nightclub the Zomba Café in Studio City, California, which later became Oil Can Harry's and then the Write-Off Room. I had known Aunt Paula was also a dancer, but, as with

Grandma Sheila, I'd never questioned her career, until now. I was astounded by these latest revelations. I guess moments of truth have a way of making you feel undone, as if the ground beneath you has shifted. I needed to know more, to be able to wrap my head around the fact that my grandmother was indeed a "stripper." So, I decided to do some research on burlesque to better understand the industry.

Sheila

The French word *burlesque* originated from the Italian word *burlesco*, which is derived from *burla*, meaning a joke, ridicule, or mockery—to laugh at or to make fun of. This sounded interesting so far, I thought.

I started reading a book called *Burlesque: Legendary Stars of the Stage*, by Jane Briggeman. Not far in, I read about a well-known dancer named Jennie Lee, "The Bazoom Girl," who just so happened to work alongside another dancer named Rusty Lane

—my Aunt Paula! I couldn't believe Aunt Paula's name and photograph were in Briggeman's book, which I owned!

Jennie Lee and Rusty Lane had performed at some of the same nightclubs in Los Angeles and were a part of the Exotic Dancers League (EDL), which they formed alongside seven other well-known dancers in 1955. These nine women advocated for higher wages, better working conditions, and fair practices for the dancers.

By 1957, Rusty Lane had become the organization's vice president and was reelected for a second term. The girls in the EDL also formed a softball team, and my aunt batted and played in the outfield at Griffith Park, where all their games were held. I even found an article with a picture of all the girls on the ballfield holding catchers' mitts. It was such fun to discover these new insights about Aunt Paula and the industry she was very much a part of. But I was just scratching the surface, and I wanted to learn more...

Further in Briggeman's book, there is a quote by Jennie Lee, who describes what it meant to be a burlesque dancer. She confidently stated, "Stripping is an art. It's more than boobs and bottoms. You've got to have beauty of face, a figure and talent. A good stripper has to master the art of the tease. She has to have a well-planned act that leaves the audience calling for 'more' without becoming crude or vulgar. You also have to have showmanship, poise, and publicity. You're a professional entertainer."

Grandma Sheila and Aunt Paula far exceeded these qualities. From my memories, Aunt Paula was fabulous, with beautiful red hair, charm, and a great figure. Grandma Sheila was stunningly beautiful from head to toe and had an amazing voice and a bold, charismatic personality that brought joy and laughter to everyone around her.

As I continued my research, I learned that burlesque, true to its root name, encompassed an entire variety show, showcasing exceptional talent, brilliant humor, and originality that appealed to many audiences, even people who didn't understand the English language. The comedians were actually said to be the biggest part of the show, more so than the dancers. But burlesque was all-around entertaining because the music was so spectacular and all the performers were so talented, elegant, animated, and alive, as well as clever and funny. You didn't need to understand the language to enjoy the show.

"Burlesque for centuries has been a legitimate branch of show business," Ann Corio stated in her book, *This Was Burlesque*. What burlesque was *not*? It was not full nudity. It was not prostitution or sleazy dances on a dirty pole in some dive bar. It was not a gentlemen-only club. It was a huge production that involved dancers, comedians, actors, musicians, and stage directors. The theaters and nightclubs were filled with couples. In another book, *The Bare Truth: Stars of Burlesque from the '40s and '50s*, by Len Rothe, I read a description of what a typical burlesque show might have entailed and how it followed a specific format, which I've paraphrased below:

> A full orchestra would play music to hush the anxiously waiting audience before the curtain opened to a line of chorus dancers. This was followed by a comedy routine and a singer's performance. A "cooch" dancer, who did contortions, or sometimes a "shimmy" dancer might do a routine, reminding the crowd of what was to follow. Next, there was a short dramatic sketch, before the chorus girls took the stage again. Then another hilarious comedy scene would be followed by a team of acrobats closing out the first half of the show.
>
> After an intermission, the second half would start off similar to the first, but with shorter acts, and it ended with

the headline stripteaser who performed for about seven to eight minutes. This portion of the show was all about the tasteful and lavish art of the *tease*—not the strip. And just like the rest of the performances, the striptease was also only an act—sometimes combined with a brilliant narrative blending seduction with intelligent humor.

As I kept on with my research, I came across another article that had been published in multiple newspapers in 1957, about Rusty Lane teaching pupils at a "school for strippers" in Hollywood. In this article, Aunt Paula also stated that "stripteasing is an art—every little gesture means something." While coaching a dancer named Toddy, she mentioned how she was trying to break Toddy of the bad habit of removing her clothing and swinging it at the audience. She stressed to the women that when they do that, "it doesn't have dignity," because striptease was not about *just* taking your clothes off. The act was to be a form of art.

I was thrilled to have found this archive about my aunt's teaching and found it moving to read her words firsthand: it really made her work come alive for me. I also had a very nice conversation with a man named Jay Stollman, a musician who got his first official job at the Emerald Room in 1971 as a drummer. During our phone call, Jay briefly described the environment of the Emerald Room. He mentioned how the patrons were dressed up in the finest clothing and that the Emerald Room was a "real" nightclub, "a classy, clean, dinner theater show with several acts." He even described how the wooden dance floor, which was directly in front of the band, was on a hydraulic system that would be raised up during some of the performances. The Emerald Room and Sound View Hotel no longer exist, which to me made it more remarkable to talk with someone who worked at the same club as Grandma Sheila. This encounter served as an additional affirmation of the artistry of burlesque, even fifteen years after Grandma Sheila left the club. In the book and documentary film *Behind the Burly Q*, Leslie Zemekis writes, "No one goes to a strip club today to see an elaborate production. Patrons are there for nudity, not for entertainment." Aunt Paula's younger daughter, Joy, told me that Aunt Paula and Grandma Sheila visited a strip club for fun one evening on Sunset Boulevard in the 1980s. They were completely appalled by what they saw and never went back. It was no longer burlesque.

As I continued combing through all sorts of books, articles, and documentaries, it became evident to me that burlesque was genuine entertainment, and the comedians and dancers in these shows were adored just as any Hollywood star. In fact, with the industry being so tough to break into, many Hollywood stars had started their careers in burlesque and vaudeville shows: Gypsy Rose, Sally Rand, Ann Corio, Abbott and Costello, Jackie Gleason, and Danny Kaye, to name a few.

And then there was Rusty Lane, a burlesque legend. Through my research, I learned that in addition to dancing nationwide and teaching pupils how to dance, Aunt Paula had starred in a musical comedy film called *Sideshow Burlesque*. She'd also coached actresses like Barbara Nichols during her role as a stripper in a two-part drama called *The Untouchables*. Aunt Paula loved to dance and officially retired at the age of fifty—her last show was in Las Vegas, according to Joy. After retiring, she traveled with her husband, Richard Benedict, my Uncle Pepe, who was an actor and director (perhaps best known for his role in the original *Ocean's Eleven* movie). Joy said her mother stayed in touch with many of the girls in the industry, and I wondered if Grandma Sheila kept in contact with any girls when she left the industry.

Aunt Paula, aka Rusty Lane (courtesy of Rusty Lane)

Aunt Paula lived with Joy and Joy's husband during her final year, as they provided her with care. She passed away peacefully at the age of ninety-one in Glenwood Springs, Colorado, in Joy's arms. Aunt Paula had three children and two grandchildren, whom I am close to. She was deeply loved by many. Joy, who is her last living child, wanted to share that Aunt Paula was "the best mother in the whole world, generous and loving," and that she misses "her beautiful soul every day." Maybe one day I'll find Sheila Lind or Rusty Lane in the Burlesque Hall of Fame museum in Las Vegas. I haven't visited the museum yet, but I plan to.

While the burlesque industry went through ups and downs and transformations because of its controversy and censorship, the peak of the golden days of burlesque (the 1920s through the 1960s) remains a big part of American culture and history. This branch of show business was known as an American art form, and it provided a livelihood for the many people involved in its production—performers, ushers, producers, waiters, stagehands. Even the candy concessioners were able to earn a salary from it. Many women were also given the chance to escape poverty, abuse, and limited opportunities. Burlesque comedy alone was also a beloved form of entertainment that was woven into American life. Even as I write this, I can't help but agree with others about the clever genius behind Abbott and Costello's classic skit, "Who's on First?"

Despite my initial reservations about the striptease aspect, I gained a richer understanding of burlesque that allowed me to appreciate why Grandpa Jack had been so supportive of Grandma Sheila's career during the golden days of burlesque. Grandma Sheila and Aunt Paula were remarkable women, in both character and appearance, possessing an abundance of talent that deserves to be remembered.

Still, even with this new knowledge, I wasn't any closer to uncovering whether Grandpa Jack had known he wasn't my mother's biological father. A sense of frustration still ate at me as I continued with my search for answers. Why couldn't someone just tell us?! The unanswered question hung over me, and I would not stop until I found the whole truth.

CHAPTER FOURTEEN: MARYANN

APRIL 2018

After speaking to Dana multiple times on the phone since February, it was now time to talk to Maryann, the second of the three cousins I'd met on Ancestry. Speaking to strangers, albeit ones I was related to, was still new territory to me. I found it so uncomfortable, especially because of all the questions I wanted to ask. It was an emotional minefield: I really wanted information and answers, but I also didn't want to say the wrong thing and upset anyone.

It was a sunny afternoon and I was in my home office when I called Maryann, who was in her mid-seventies at the time. She greeted me gently and spoke with a soft, careful tone that instantly brought me a sense of calm. It was a short but delightful conversation. Maryann shared that she was in Arizona, where she lived during that time of the year as a "snowbird." Her home is surprisingly very close to where my mother currently lives in Arizona! The rest of the year she lived in New Jersey.

During our conversation, Maryann told me she'd always suspected her mother Nettie was one of Nino's siblings who knew about my mother's existence.

Nettie	—	Grace	—	Nino	—	*(siblings)*
|		|		|		
Maryann		James		Mom		(1C)
		|		|		
		Dana		Me/Rebecca		(2C)

"So, I wanted to let you know that I have all of my mother Nettie's photo albums," Maryann said. "I had a vague memory of her showing me a picture of my Uncle Nino with a little girl many years ago, and she said it was his daughter. At the time, I didn't think to ask anything about it—I was young. But ever since then I've wondered who that daughter was. And then with Ancestry, I started to think maybe I could find her."

"Oh wow! Do you think that photograph could be in one of the albums you have?" I asked.

"Well, that's what I wanted to tell you . . . So Nino died in March 2001, and my mother actually inherited all of his personal items and albums. Which *I* inherited after she passed six months later."

Oh my goodness, really? My mind raced. This meant that Maryann possessed not only Nettie's albums but all of her Uncle Nino's personal photographs and belongings! Maryann had just become a key person in my search.

I couldn't hold back my excitement. "Maryann, do you think you'd mind going through his belongings to see if he has any records of my mother? Or your mother's albums?"

"No, not at all. I was actually going to suggest that I look through everything," she said. "There's just one hiccup . . . My mother's and Nino's albums are in boxes at my home in New Jersey and I'm in Arizona now. I don't go back home to New Jersey until after Memorial Day at the end of May," she said.

Oh no! It was only April!

The suspense would be unbearable! We were on the verge of

gaining new information about my grandmother and my new biological grandfather, and we had to WAIT?!

Waiting. Is. Hard.

These potential items could unlock so much for us. I may have been foolish to believe she could find anything important, but I had to hold on to hope as I continued my search for the whole truth. I knew there was still a chance that the boxes would be full of photos that were unrelated to us, or maybe there'd be no photos at all, just some old trinkets. Either way, we wouldn't know for sure until Maryann could get back to Jersey and go through everything. But I was optimistic, and so was my mom once I shared this new piece of information with her.

Maryann said she'd never looked through Nettie's old photos before, or explored the items that belonged to her Uncle Nino, so who knew what she might discover? We were determined and eager to learn more about the connection between Nino and Sheila, and Maryann might hold the key.

In the meantime, we could hardly contain ourselves!

CHAPTER FIFTEEN: DISCOVERY

MAY–JULY 2018

Time had dragged since my conversation with Maryann, as we waited for Memorial Day, when she'd said she'd be back in New Jersey. In early May, my nephew was born and we were all overjoyed to welcome him to the world. It was a long-awaited moment for us, and his birth gave my mom a new purpose. She was now "Grammie" to her third beautiful grandchild.

Memorial Day came and went, and we hadn't heard back from Maryann yet. Though we didn't want to pressure her, by June the suspense was killing us. In need of some distraction, my mom and sister decided to visit my house in July for a few days. It would be my nephew's first time on an airplane. I could hardly wait to snuggle him again.

As happy as I was to see them, the visit began with some sad news. The day after my mom, sister, and nephew arrived, Dad, who'd stayed home to care for Grandma Lorraine, called to tell us she had passed away. The last time I'd seen her was shortly after my nephew's birth when my kids and I went to visit her. She was just shy of ninety and in great spirits that day. Rebecca was there, too, and Grandma Lorraine was overjoyed to meet her great-grandson.

Dad said he and his youngest sister had been by Grandma Lorraine's side as she died in her sleep at the home where she raised her family. Grandma Lorraine had a gold necklace that read "39 and Holding," that my parents gave to her and she often wore. After she passed, my dad sent her necklace to me because I was also "39 and Holding" that year. That day at my home, as Mom, Rebecca, and I celebrated Grandma Lorraine's life, I reflected on what a wonderful grandmother she was to me. I felt grateful to have her family history and memories safely stored in my files.

On the third day of their trip, we were enjoying a warm day out by the pool with my kids and the baby. I'd been taking pictures of Rebecca and my nephew in the water. Rebecca reminded me so much of Grandma Sheila—the way Grandma used to hold us and swim with us. It was precious. My mom was sitting in the shade when her phone rang.

It was Maryann—at last!

I ran over to where Mother was sitting on one of the loungers, and Rebecca followed, dripping water, with the baby in her arms. She put her phone on speaker so we could listen as Maryann explained how she was finally back home in New Jersey and had just started searching through the closet where Nino's boxes were stored.

"I think I may have found something," she said. "But I have to tell you, it was very interesting the way I made this discovery. The way I found the photos..."

Rebecca clutched my arm as I looked at her. *Photos?*

"Really? Do tell!" my mom said.

"So, I was looking up high in the closet with a flashlight when I dropped the flashlight and it landed on my foot. I got kind of upset because it hurt a lot. But when I bent down to get the flashlight, I noticed the light shining on a white envelope near my foot. I was confused where the envelope came from because I didn't remember seeing it down there before. So I picked it up, and when I opened the envelope, I found a stack of pictures..."

I was holding my breath as Maryann continued.

"There are photos of Nino when he was younger. And he's holding an infant... a baby girl."

"Oh wow!" we said in chorus, looking at one another with big eyes.

"Do you recognize the girl?" I asked.

"No, but there are lots of photos here of Nino with the same girl," Maryann went on. "There's one where she's about one or two years old, and there's a couple with a young boy, too. I don't recognize him either. So... I'm assuming the little girl is you, Michelle? There's also a couple of greeting cards here."

"Oh my gosh, oh my gosh, oh my gosh!" we shouted in unison. *Surely these had to be photos of Nino with my mom?*

"I'll take pictures and text them to you right now so you can make sure it's you. Let me hang up and I'll start doing that."

"Okay, oh my gosh, yes, thank you!" Mom said.

"And if it's you, I can put the originals in the mail," she added.

I think all of our hearts were pounding out of our chests at this point. It had been a long three months waiting for Maryann, but this was more than we could have hoped for.

Minutes later, Mom's phone pinged as the digital images started pouring in.

Rebecca and I hung over her shoulder to see the photos.

The first image came up, and Mom yelled, "Oh my gosh, that's me!" She zoomed in on the screen so we could see the photo of a baby girl. I couldn't believe it... There she was! My mother, in Nino's arms. It was indisputably her! We were all astounded.

The next picture showed a young boy—Steven, my mother's older brother! The age seemed right: he looked about five years old in the photo, and he was holding on to my mother from behind. There were also a couple photos of Nino on a sidewalk in town, smiling and wearing dark slacks, shiny shoes, and a short-sleeved, button-down shirt. My mom, who appears to be a little over a year old, is standing barefoot in a dress beside a stroller, holding Nino's hand. We guessed this photo had been taken somewhere in the Bronx, where Nino lived.

Mom swiped to the next picture, one of Grandma Sheila wearing dark pants, a white tank top, and strappy flat sandals.

With her hair tied back in a handkerchief, she was smiling while standing in the same spot as Nino, on the same sidewalk in town.

There were several more pictures of my mother as a newborn and Nino holding my mother as a toddler, in different settings.

And then the most telling photo appeared...

Grandma Sheila and Nino are both barefoot on the beach, their hands intertwined. You can see the boardwalk behind them. Nino is shirtless and smiling, and Grandma Sheila is smiling, too ... and displaying a significant pregnancy under her white tank top and dark-colored shorts! She was carrying my mother!

Our jaws dropped.

"Ohhh, my gosh!" Mom's eyes were wide with surprise.

Rebecca and I exchanged glances. I could see she was as stunned as me.

Nino and Sheila, 1954

And there were more surprises to come: in addition to the photos, there were a few handwritten items. We recognized the cursive handwriting immediately. It was Grandma Sheila's.

The first was a Father's Day card. We were back inside the

house now, at the kitchen table. I reached over Mom's shoulder to zoom in on the screen.

"For Dad on Father's Day . . ." I read. "To a dad who's really top-notch, a champion through and through—here's wishes for a year of luck, and happiness in all you do! From Michelle and Steven."

Rebecca and I watched as Mom swiped to the next screen displaying a note that appeared to be written on the back of the Father's Day card. I read it out loud:

"'Hello Honey . . . I hope you like the shirts I sent. We are all fine and we miss you very much. Everything is coming along. This is just a short note, I'll write again this week . . . The baby cut two more teeth. I'll write more in my letter. I love you and miss you. Have a nice day dear. XXXX. Love always, Sheila.'"

This note was followed by a Christmas card, which I read, too: "'To my sweetheart. Upon this grand old holiday, may joy be yours anew. And may each day that passes by hold happiness for you. I'll love you always, Sheila.' . . . Wow! 'I'll love you always' . . . These are written with so much love and affection, but what did she mean by 'everything is coming along'?" I asked.

"I have no idea." Mom was in a daze, still swiping back and forth through the images.

"Maybe Nino was the 'Italian man' she tried to 'run off with' back then? Maybe they were planning to be together?" Rebecca said.

The three of us still wonder what Grandma Sheila meant by that statement.

As I watched my mother swipe through the photos and letters again, I thought about what they revealed about Nino and Grandma Sheila's relationship. Clearly, there was a strong love between them. The dates of the pictures and the postmarked cards indicated that their relationship carried on for at least two years, then ended abruptly. This meant my mother never truly knew the man who was her biological father. He had held her for only a moment in time before disappearing from her life. But why?

Did his disappearance have anything to do with the story of Grandpa Jack pulling a gun on a man and telling him to stay away from his family?

Nevertheless, even if we never found out the full story, it was comforting to find out that she indeed came from love.

Moreover, we found it very significant that Nino kept the pictures and letters for all those years . . . as if he was hoping that one day, they would make a full circle back to my mother. And they did. After almost sixty-four years, they were now in her hands.

A few days later, after she and Rebecca got back home, Mom called her brother Steven again to ask if he remembered anything from that time, seeing as he was in several of their photos. He was very surprised to learn about this. He searched his memory and said he actually did recall their mother being with a man. As a young child, he'd never thought much of it, though, because every day Grandma Sheila and Grandpa Jack would meet and hang out with different people.

After seeing the photographic proof of Grandma Sheila and Nino's relationship and speaking to Steven, it still took my mother time to process everything. She told me how bewildered she felt. Though the old photos were black and white, they felt to her as if they were in full color.

"It's crushing in one way and validating in another," she told my sister and me.

Weeks turned into months as we slowly came to terms with our new truth. Throughout that time, I kept in continuous contact with Dana. She and I were growing closer, and we were eager to meet each other. We felt strongly about having a family reunion, and Mom, who'd become increasingly more curious, was also open to the idea. So, Dana reached out to her side of the family, while I spoke to mine. Eight months later, Mom and I were on a Southwest flight headed to Florida to meet the cousins who'd been longing to find her.

Sixty-four years later, thanks to Maryann holding on to her childhood memory, their time had finally come...

CHAPTER SIXTEEN: FLORIDA

The time had come! It was March 2019, and Mom and I were on our way to Florida. Rebecca sadly couldn't join us because her son was only ten months old, so it was just Mom and me.

I was beyond excited to meet everyone, especially Dana. I almost couldn't believe I was finally going to meet her in person! From the first phone call, Dana and I had hit it off and were immediately comfortable with each other, and in the weeks leading up to our visit, we had spent countless hours on the phone, sometimes talking through the night. We had a million stories to catch up on. Obviously! It felt as if we'd known each other for a lifetime. Our conversations flowed so naturally, and we had so much in common. My husband would laugh when he'd pass by after several hours and I was *still* on the phone. He knew exactly who I was talking to! Dana's husband reacted the same way. They knew we needed this visit, to meet. We had way too many years to catch up on.

In total, Mom and I would meet thirteen new family members! Nine cousins along with four spouses. The only ones we knew already were the three cousins we'd met through

Ancestry, the culprits who made this all happen—Dana, Maryann, and Dana's father James, aka Jimmy.

The first cousin we met was Jimmy's younger brother, Mike. We spent our first night at Mike and his wife Irene's lovely home. The next day, Jimmy and Maryann arrived. Maryann, who'd sent us all the photos and letters between Nino and my grandmother, was now standing in front of us! It was surreal. Jimmy and Mike's sisters, Toni and Trudy, stopped by to meet us, too. Overwhelmed with excitement was an understatement.

That evening we spent a short time talking, but it was getting late and we were expected early the next day at Jimmy's home, where a few more cousins would meet us—including Dana, who was flying in the next day. My mother and I shared a bed, and I recall sleeping very well that evening. After all the months of waiting and wondering, all the shocks and upsets, for the first time in a long time, I finally felt at peace.

The next day we drove to Jimmy and his wife Joann's home. (This was Joann without an *e*—later we'd meet a Joanne with an *e*, too!) Toni and Trudy arrived shortly after us, and finally Dana.

I was outside on the back patio with everyone when Dana walked in . . . all my emotions fully surfaced and I burst into tears. Happy tears. I knew instantly who she was. We grabbed each other and couldn't let go. We were both in tears. The best way to describe it was like I'd lost someone I loved that I never thought I would see again, and then suddenly there she was. I was flooded with so much joy, I felt my heart could burst. We were meant to be family. I absolutely adore her. I couldn't physically let go of her through the tears, but we finally moved apart and began to talk. I remember looking around and seeing everyone smiling at us.

When we discussed sleeping arrangements, I was selfishly relieved to hear that Dana and I would be staying together at the same house, with her father Jimmy and his wife Joann. Everyone knew we would want to stay together. I asked my mother how she felt about it, and she was just fine not having to share a bed with me. Ha! Dana and I slept in a room with two twin-sized beds. I felt like a little girl on a campout. We sat on our beds each night and talked until the sun rose and we could no longer keep our eyes open. We did our hair and makeup together in the shared bathroom. It was so precious and so much fun. She truly feels like another sister to me.

Joann cooked us authentic Italian dishes that were so delicious! Italian sausage bread, lasagna, and many yummy desserts—Italian rice pudding, pizzelle, zeppole, biscotti, and more. She shared the recipes of each dish, and I have them added to my own family recipe book now. I learned that ricotta is key. No wonder I love ricotta so much! A couple of close family friends who knew Nino very well joined us later for dinner. As they talked about him, they kept saying how much they "loved that guy." Everyone who spoke of Nino loved him. It was so nice to hear their perspectives.

The following day, we were taken around to some Florida sites. We went to the beautiful Historic Spanish Point where we took pictures by the water. Later that evening, we went out for dinner where we not only ate but also danced to live music. I remember sitting at the table watching my mother having the time of her life dancing with her newest cousins to "Wooly Bully" and other fun songs. I watched them hold on to one another as they laughed and kicked their legs around before jumping into a train and moving through the dance floor together. I thought, *My mother deserves this . . . My cousins deserve this*. Nothing had been in their control before. But it was now. And no one could separate them any longer. They were going to hold on and love one another from this moment on, no matter what.

On my last evening in Florida, Toni and her husband Joe hosted a lovely afternoon, and we got to meet three more cousins. Joanne (with an *e*) flew in from New York, and Donna and Denise, fraternal twins, traveled from Fort Myers and Pennsylvania, respectively. Their oldest sister Dede couldn't make it but FaceTimed with us.

Before dinner, we sat in the living room listening to story after story about Nino from everyone. The first was about Nino's black poodle, Rickey, who got mixed up at the groomer's. Mike laughed as he recounted that Nino accidentally picked up the wrong dog, not realizing it until after his grandma told Nino it wasn't Rickey. Nino thought she was crazy, but she was actually right . . . The frantic groomer finally got in touch, and they were able to return the dogs to their rightful owners. This event was so entertaining that it even made the papers in the late 1950s, according to Mike.

Nino and Autilia reunited with Rickey

We learned that Nino had lived most of his younger years in

the Bronx, New York, before moving to Englewood Cliffs, New Jersey. He served in the U.S. Army, and his family lived in a funeral parlor that they operated in the Bronx, on Morris Avenue. Nino and his mother lived on the first floor, and his siblings and their children lived on the second floor. I was told that my great-grandmother, Autilia, actually embalmed the bodies. When I was a kid, we lived down the street from a funeral home, and every time Ana, Rebecca, and I rode our bikes past the building and saw a hearse, it freaked us out. But not my Italian family! They were busy embalming bodies! The contrast still amuses me.

I was also amused by how everyone was talking, or shouting, over one another. It was chaos. Mom and I couldn't keep up! At one point I looked at Dana and she just shrugged her shoulders and laughed, too. Donna managed to wedge her voice into the noise to tell us that Nino had also worked as an "office boy" and a chauffeur. She said that Nino used to play tennis with her from time to time, and he would send her to the store to pick up his favorite Montecristo cigars. Mike and Jimmy said Nino would tip the neighborhood kids $20 for buying him cigars, and the kids fought to get picked. They also shared that Nino always drove the best cars, most notably a black Cadillac, and he used to hang out at a bar called the Step Up Tavern off 52nd Street, which I read was at the epicenter of the New York jazz scene in the 1950s.

Next, Toni and Trudy shared that in the 1960s Nino and his girlfriend at the time took them on a road trip to Spartanburg, South Carolina. Toni and Trudy had grown up in the Bronx, surrounded by apartments, tenements, and one lonesome tree that stood in front of the family home on Morris Avenue, so they could hardly imagine what they'd see after leaving the city, which was all they'd known up until that point in their lives.

"Our eyes were opened wide when we arrived at the most

magnificent home," Toni said. "It felt like a mansion. We also witnessed segregation for the first time on this trip. We couldn't understand why Black people were separated at the fountains and bathrooms, partly because we were so young, and where we came from in the Bronx, everyone was allowed to be together. It didn't make any sense to us." It was a sad point in time, but also a very memorable experience for them—one that, as Nino had hoped, opened their eyes and hearts to the world outside the city.

Donna told us how she'd planned for Nino to walk her down the aisle when she got married in 1993, but unfortunately, Nino got sick and lost his leg due to a blood clot. Sadly, he never made it to her wedding at all. Toni took out some photos of Nino in his elderly years, with a prosthetic.

"Nino was a jokester and scared my daughter once when he sat down and took off his leg! He called the leg his 'prostitute,'" Denise said as she laughed. Mom and I laughed, too. Nino was well cared for by fellow family members as he adjusted to being disabled.

After the photos, Joe put on a DVD. It was an old 8mm film from 1968 of my great-grandmother Autilia's eightieth birthday party. Trudy, who told us that she had been behind the camera, narrated for Mom and me so we knew who everyone was.

The film began with footage of the guests mingling, then moved on to the meal. Everyone was smiling as they ate at long, rectangular, banquet-style tables. One of Nino's brothers, Frank, slow danced with Maryann, then let go of her and broke into a serious impression of what looked like "The Nitty Gritty" dance, then burst out laughing. It was heartwarming to witness everyone's abundant love for Autilia. The joyful expressions, the hugs, the dancing. Toward the end, though there was no sound, you could tell they were singing "Happy Birthday" to her. As they sang she stood motioning like a conductor, holding a cake knife in her right hand as she waited to cut her cake, which read,

"Happy Birthday Mother." Following the cake-cutting, family members lined up to give Autilia a goodbye kiss, starting with the children and women.

Even though I couldn't hear their words, their smiles and body language said it all. It looked like a very warm party. Autilia immigrated from Italy in 1908 and passed away in 1981 at the age of 92. She outlived her husband Antonio, who passed away at around the age of 67. They were one big happy family—and *still were*, I thought, as I looked around.

Next, we watched an old home video with footage that included Nino singing and showing everyone his apartment in Florida. He had an astounding voice. Deep and full. One clip showed Nino reclining on a lounge chair in someone's backyard, wearing a white shirt and light blue pants with white shoes. He's pretending to drink alcohol out of a brown Coppertone lotion bottle with his nephew, PJ, who is just a boy in the video. They are tilting the bottles in an exaggerated motion to act like they're guzzling a drink. The next moment, Donna asks Nino to sing her a song, and without any hesitation or delay he immediately sings the words, "I don't know why I love you like I do . . . sweetheart sends a letter of goodbye . . ." Then he breaks off into humming the tune humorously with his mouth turned down—"whah, whah, whah, whah . . . whah, whah, whahhh . . ."—and smiles. The tune sounded like Dean Martin's "I Don't Know Why (I Just Do)."

At that moment, I could almost picture Nino and Grandma Sheila singing together. I also couldn't help but wonder if he was singing those lyrics about her. I heard repeatedly that Nino also used to sing the lyrics "Michelle, ma belle" *all* the time. Everyone in the family had always assumed he was singing this about Dana's sister, Michelle. Or had it been for his daughter, Michelle? Or for both of them? We'll never truly know.

Nino was also known for being a huge Frank Sinatra fan and was always singing Sinatra songs. He had a fairly large collection of Sinatra records in his Florida apartment and a large framed poster of Sinatra on his wall. In one part of the home videos, the camera takes the viewer on a tour of Nino's home, through his front door into his kitchen, where Nino, Dede, and Donna, who is behind the camera, talk about a *tray-ceiling* remodel he'd done. It proceeds to his living room and ends up in his bedroom, where PJ is pretending to talk on an antique phone Nino has on his nightstand. His home is tidy and elegantly furnished, with white sofas, a glass dining table, and a hutch full of assorted glassware. In the yellow-and-white kitchen, every utensil is neatly hung in its place. It appeared that he lived alone in this apartment.

By the end of the viewing, my mother and I were emotionally overloaded, to say the least. The videos and our cousins' recollections really brought Nino to life for us. They stopped at nothing when it came to sharing all the wonderful character traits they'd cherished so much about him: "Nino was one of a kind and had a heart of gold." He clearly was the "cool uncle" who enriched all of their lives, and it was evident he'd loved all of them fiercely.

I really wish I could have met Nino.

After dinner, we sat around Toni's large dining room table sharing more stories and laughs. Then the cousins gathered around my mother. With tears in their eyes, Joanne, Donna, and Denise handed her a box.

"Michelle, this was something that Nino gave our mother," Joanne said as Mom opened the box. Inside was a sparkling, triangle-shaped diamond pendant set in white gold on a white-gold chain.

Joanne explained, "Many years ago, Nino gave this same necklace as a gift not only to our mother but to ALL the women of the family. His sisters and his sisters-in-law all got one." One being their mother, Madeline, to whom this necklace had belonged.

Joanne continued, "Nino gave it with so much love to the women in our family, and it only makes sense for you to have this necklace now, Michelle. It's a small piece of his love that we can finally pass to you."

This moment was completely unexpected. They had already been so loving and welcoming, and then this happened. I couldn't hold back my tears any longer. I glanced over at my mom, who was speechless as tears streamed down her face, too. She was so humbled that at first, she hesitated to receive this treasured sentiment from them, saying, "No, I can't take your mother's necklace from Nino."

Joanne immediately insisted, "My sisters and I all agreed that *you* need to have it—and if our mother was here, she would have wanted you to have it! And if you were around when your father Nino was alive, we know he would have given you one of your own. You probably would have been the first person to get one. So really, it belongs to you, Michelle. Please take it and wear it and know how much love it carries."

There wasn't a single dry eye at the table—even the men were crying. It was the most touching moment of the trip, and I'll never forget it. I imagined how proud Nino would have felt about them passing on this treasured and heartwarming memento to my mother. She wears it to this day.

Not only was the necklace beautiful, but the shape captivated me.

A triangle: three points.

Watching Joanne put the necklace around Mom's neck, I was suddenly struck.

She had three parents.

Three hearts that loved her dearly, and I began to cry again.

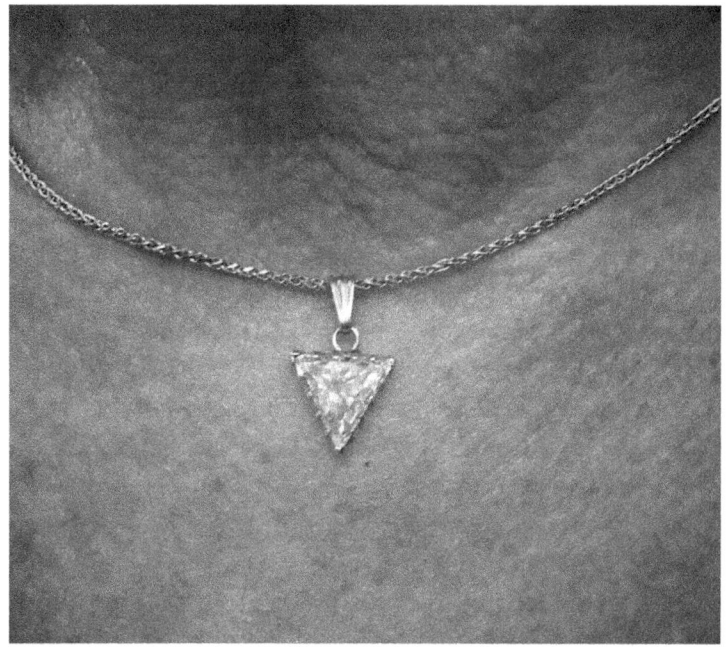

Nino's necklace, given to Mom

I had to get back to my family, but Mom stayed in Florida for a few more days after I left. Later she told me how she rode in Donna's boat, watched sunsets, went to dinners, and made everlasting bonds with her new cousins. She'd also started to watch an Italian series, *My Brilliant Friend*, with Toni while staying at her house.

I heard that on her last day, Mom gave a heartwarming speech to her cousins in which she said she was blessed to be kissed on the cheek by both of her fathers. She also expressed her enormous gratitude and appreciation to everyone. The speech was filmed, and it was so precious for me to watch the video of her talking to them around a table at a restaurant.

It was a trip neither of us will ever forget, filled with tears of joy and endless hugs and kisses from everyone, from the moment we arrived until the day we left.

I remember flying home and trying to process everything. My head was still in a whirlwind. At forty years old, I'd just spent an extended weekend with a whole new part of my family that I never even knew existed. We ate, we danced, we laughed, we cried, we loved. I held back my tears all the way home. Tears of pure joy and fulfillment. I felt relieved and comforted knowing that my mother was in good hands and loved beyond measure. It completely filled my heart. It was truly the happiest ending to what could have been a completely heartbreaking story.

Once I got home and settled in, the pain in my leg arrived with a fury. I ended up having my second surgery two weeks later for a severely bulged disc in my back. While in recovery, I was contacted for a second time by a newly found cousin, a woman named Patti who was still searching for her birth father. We had briefly corresponded months earlier, but I wasn't emotionally ready to dive into another family debacle at the time, so I had continued to put off my response to her. Little did I know, a treasure was waiting for me . . .

CHAPTER SEVENTEEN: AUTUMN LEAVES

JUNE 2019

Once I'd recovered from surgery at the start of summer break, Rebecca, Mom, the kids, and I took a trip to visit Aunt Jean. She had moved to San Diego a few years ago to be closer to her daughters. It was wonderful to be able to visit her more often now that we lived in the same state.

After spending a chilly day at the beach, we arrived at Aunt Jean's house. The plan was to take some pictures of her and the three children, but getting my nephew, who'd recently turned one and had just started walking, to hold still for the photos was nearly impossible—and quite comical! Adorable and wiggly, he kept squirming in her arms and sliding down to the floor. Aunt Jean was very understanding and just laughed at the situation.

Abandoning the photo shoot, we spent the rest of the afternoon chatting in Aunt Jean's living room. I can't recall exactly how it came up, but at some point, she mentioned how Grandma Sheila used to sing a song called "Autumn Leaves" by Frank Sinatra.

No kidding, I thought. *Frank Sinatra?*

"Your grandmother *loved* that song," Aunt Jean continued.

"She sang it *all* the time. You know she had the most beautiful voice."

I was both grateful and intrigued that Aunt Jean had shared this memory with me. It resonated with everything I knew about Grandma Sheila's background in performing—how everyone was always telling me what a beautiful voice she'd had, and Grandpa Jack used to say that, along with Eve Arden and Ethel Merman, she could have been the next Judy Garland. But Aunt Jean's comment also got me thinking more about Frank Sinatra . . . *Nino used to sing Frank Sinatra, too. Interesting.* And there went my brain again . . . spinning round and round.

As soon as I got home from visiting Aunt Jean, I searched for the song and listened to it. I wanted to feel the song. I wanted to picture her singing it. Why did she love this song so much? What sort of connection did she have with it?

Listening to "Autumn Leaves," I was astounded by its beauty and tragedy. The song is a dark lament of lost love, regret, and the passing of time. It took me right to the 1950s and, unexpectedly, to Nino. To me, the lyrics perfectly captured the essence of their brief love story.

As I sat on my living room sofa, I thought of all the photographs I'd seen of Nino and Grandma Sheila together, in which it was so clear how in love they were. Then I thought of the line in the song about holding sunburned hands: several pictures showed the two of them at the beach holding hands, like the one in which Grandma Sheila was pregnant. My mom was in many of these beach photos, too. It's no wonder she loves the beach and sunshine, I thought. She was born into it.

As I kept replaying the song, I recalled the Christmas card where Grandma Sheila had written, "I'll love you always," and then that cryptic line in the Father's Day card: "Everything is coming along." September 1955 was the date on the photos

Grandma Sheila mailed to Nino after my mother's first birthday, the month before, and there were no more photos after this. Was that the end of their relationship? And what happened? Could that have been when Grandpa Jack found out about their relationship? Or did Nino and Grandma Sheila mutually agree to end things? And if not, who left whom? I thought of the part in the song about "my darling" going away and the days growing longer, and how they're missed . . . I wondered, *Why did Aunt Jean decide to share this information with me now? Was it really just a coincidence?* I couldn't stop thinking about the links between the song and Grandma Sheila and Nino's relationship . . .

A few years before, I'd started taking piano lessons for the first time in my life. My piano teacher, Jian, always chose pieces that really challenged me, and as my skills matured, I learned to play arrangements of Mozart minuets, portions of Beethoven pieces, and a couple of Chopin's preludes, among other pieces. Maybe I could play "Autumn Leaves," too! I asked Jian if he could help, and he found the perfect intermediate arrangement that was appropriate for my skill level.

This song would end up being my grand finale to piano lessons, because right after I finished it, COVID hit, Jian moved out of state, and my lessons ended.

I recently read that the original song was written in French and called "Les Feuilles Mortes," which literally means "dead leaves." In 1950, the song was translated to English and given a gentler title, "Autumn Leaves," which reached No. 1, according to *Billboard* magazine, after being recorded by Roger Williams. Throughout the 1950s, many leading pop vocalists and jazz instrumentalists also recorded the song, including Frank Sinatra —so "Autumn Leaves" was certainly at its peak during the time of Grandma Sheila and Nino's affair and demise.

Now that I'm writing this book, the song "Autumn Leaves"

carries even more meaning, knowing how much Grandma Sheila loved it. I am so thankful Jian helped me learn to play it, and whenever I do, I like to imagine that she is singing along from above.

Grandma Sheila

CHAPTER EIGHTEEN: DNA ANGEL

APRIL 2019–FEBRUARY 2021

In the midst of my investigations, another search had been going on. Seven months after my DNA discovery, in September 2018, I was contacted by a new cousin named Patti. At that time, I'd hoped she might be able to provide an explanation for my Italian heritage. We had briefly exchanged some information, and I learned that although Patti was related to me through Grandma Sheila's family, her reason for contacting me had nothing to do with my Italian DNA. Instead, Patti's connection came through my great-grandfather Izzy and the Ashkenazi Jewish Austrian side of my family.

I hadn't corresponded with Patti since our initial exchange, but I clearly remember the day I received her follow-up message in April 2019, while I was still in recovery from my surgery. My heart ached as I read the details of her story. She told me she'd been adopted as a little girl through an agency called Louise Wise Services, now Spence-Chapin Services, and was trying to find out who her birth father was. Her Ancestry search and DNA test had led her to me, but other than the fact that we were closely related cousins—through her unknown birth father—she knew nothing about the rest of my (our) Jewish maternal family. She desperately wanted to find out how she fit into a family she'd never known.

Cousin Patti

We corresponded a few times, and I wanted to keep replying, but I struggled. I just couldn't do it. I was so happy after the Florida reunion, but my wounds were still fresh, and I was still processing everything I'd just been through. I felt nowhere near mentally or emotionally ready to take this on. However, after a few weeks passed, I suddenly snapped out of it. I realized I'd actually gotten really good at this genealogy stuff and thought, *This woman was my second cousin. Why was I allowing her to go through this alone?* I had a lot of family history at my fingertips! Maybe some of the information I had could help her. I'd been fortunate enough to receive help from several people in figuring out my own story, so why shouldn't I give everything I had to help Patti? Furthermore, she told me that almost every distant family member she'd reached out to for information had turned her down. Whatever their reason, they simply didn't want to be involved. This made me so sad for her.

From then on, I made a conscious decision to fully commit to genealogy and I vowed not to stop until we solved Patti's case. I was ALL-IN. For nearly two years, I assisted Patti in searching for her father, and out of a dozen possibilities, we had narrowed it down to two men. By then, Patti had started calling me her "DNA Angel," which warmed my heart. It meant so much to be able to help her. And we were so close to finding her biological father! We often exchanged phone calls and texts to share information.

Then, in January 2021, Patti texted me that she had been in the hospital and that she was putting my phone number in her husband's book "just in case." I was concerned and asked her what was wrong. She wrote that she loved me and not to worry, but she was having some tests for her lungs the following week. I said, "OK, keep me posted" and sent her my usual virtual hug at the end of our text.

Just two weeks later, in February, I received a call from Patti's husband that she had passed away.

What?!

I was completely crushed, shocked, and heartbroken. I paced around my house struggling to keep my tears at bay, and when Nathan finally asked what was bothering me, I broke down completely. I felt stupid at first because I was weeping for a cousin I barely knew—but, I couldn't help it. I felt so connected to her, and I desperately wanted to finish the race together. I never even got to say goodbye! I felt angry and sad all over again. I couldn't understand why Patti had been brought into my life for such a short time. What was the point? Was it just to break my heart? I felt like I had completely failed.

But, there *was* a point. It was through Patti that I'd been reminded of something profound: your darkest days can be made light again. She was a gift.

Patti enriched my life immensely. Because of her story, I had been driven to investigate our Ashkenazi Jewish family, with whom she came from. In doing so, I was able to expand my family tree and connect with approximately 150 more relatives I never knew—in addition to the Italian family I'd recently inherited! I even had the chance to meet Patti's daughter on Facebook, and we continue to stay in touch to this day.

My brief two-year relationship with Patti opened up a whole new world of family for me. While we never figured out which one of the two men was her biological father (though I have my hunch), I met many additional maternal family members while helping her. I learned about great-great-grandparents, aunts, uncles, and cousins I never knew existed! This journey expanded my genealogical research and records, which in turn deepened my love for and bond with my family. I made contact with several of them, and we also stay in touch to this day.

When Patti died, Nathan and I drank a shot of bourbon and added her name to our "jar of angels," in which we keep the names of those we've lost and hold dear.

In the end, Patti was actually *my* DNA angel.

AUTUMN LEAVES

Rest in peace, Cousin Patti.

CHAPTER NINETEEN: MOM

MAY 2024

When I decided to write this story, I recognized that my mom's perspective was vital, and that sharing her voice was incredibly important, as this experience impacted her more than anyone else. I asked her to begin documenting her thoughts and feelings about this life-changing experience. Here is her heartfelt explanation, in her words:

Some people say that trauma makes you stronger; what I know is that it damages your nervous system and maybe keeps you weak. It sort of holds you hostage. The discovery of who I was and was not put me into a tailspin. I felt so much confusion, betrayal, shock, resentment, and unbelief.

How could this be true? How did I miss this growing up? Were there signs I never acknowledged? I felt stupid that so many other people knew, yet little ol' me was kept in the dark, only to find out at the age sixty-three.

I wondered what other family secrets were yet to be exposed . . .

It was a true gut punch that put me in a severe state of disorientation. There were so many sleepless nights and tears as questions flooded my mind. Why couldn't someone have blurted out the truth sooner so I could have dealt with it earlier? How could my mother walk away from her relationship of over two years and never utter Nino's name? How did she look at my face in later years and not see him? I certainly resemble him.

How could I not have known all this about my life?

I needed answers. My identity felt like a lie. After all, I grew up as a Jew of Ukrainian/Austrian and Syrian descent, and now there was no Syrian but Italian instead. To me, my birth certificate had become a perjured document. So many emotions . . .

Michelle with her parents, Sheila and Jack, circa 1958

My mother, Sheila, and I were very close and it hurt that she never told me her secret. I knew how badly my mother had wanted me and fought for her pregnancy, taking diethylstilbestrol (DES) to prevent a miscarriage. Yet she never told me who my true father was.

Although I was never really angry with my parents, and I tried to understand their side, for several months following the discovery it was very trying. In some ways, I knew that by keeping Nino and the truth around my paternity to themselves, they'd prevented me from being ostracized, bearing in mind it was the 1950s. Yet still . . .

Meanwhile, I was entering a whole new world discovering where I came from, who my paternal family was, what they were like, what genetics I might have inherited, and so on. I contacted as many of my relatives as possible to see what they knew. I wasn't even sure what questions to ask. My Uncle Al as well as Bernice and Joy were forthcoming in their answers. They immediately said "yes" to having known.

My surviving maternal Aunt Jean, however, was more reticent at first. All she would say was, "You had a good life." Not really comforting. I hadn't denied having a good life, but it wasn't a truthful life. I was never Syrian, yet I listened to their music and ate their food.

I was baffled at how many family members on my mother's side had known while, initially, it seemed no one on my father's side had any idea. That is, until I spoke to my oldest living cousin, Herbie (Bernice's brother), just before he passed away. Herbie was excited to discuss the Italian revelation and share memories of my father, Jack, with whom he'd been close over the years. He was an honest man, so I knew he wouldn't sugarcoat anything. I asked him point-blank, "Did my father know I wasn't his?"

Herbie boldly and confidently responded, "Jack wasn't stupid." Afterwards, I reflected: Herbie's statement seemed to confirm my belief that my father did know the truth. I suppose I'll never know for certain. Regardless, the fact that he never treated me differently was heartwarming. There was never a time when he made me feel like I wasn't his daughter.

I'd never had any reason to believe I didn't belong or to suspect anything was other than how it seemed. We all had brown hair and eyes, and we lived the typical middle-class life: summer sleepaway camp, beach club, Girl Scouts, and the like.

My mother raised the three of us while my father worked. He was stern with us, so we knew not to push the limits. But sometimes, we used to surprise him when he was coming home via the railroad, hiding in the back of the car. My mother would tell us when he was walking towards the car, and I would get so excited seeing the look of joy on his face.

Another memory I have was of the basement of our Rosedale house, which my parents remodeled when I was about ten years old. It looked so cool to me at the time: there was a new, built-in bar and a room for the washer/dryer. My mother had stored some of her gowns in a wardrobe, which I'd look through once in a while. Every Halloween I would dress up in Mom's long black lace dress and chandelier-type earrings to go trick-or-treating. Each year, we participated in the Trick-or-Treat for UNICEF fundraising program that began in 1950. We collected change in a small milk-container box that went towards relief funds, and I would go with her to drop off our collections the next day.

Around the same time, my father surprised me and came home with a white Fender electric guitar and a small amplifier for my weekly guitar lessons in the basement. So all in all, it was an ordinary, happy childhood and I had no reason to believe otherwise.

When I heard that a cousin of mine, Maryann, had been linked by Ancestry to my daughter, and that she was looking for me, I needed to know more. Once I got my DNA confirmation, I joined the cousins' Messenger group so they could "meet" me. They were so excited, and told me endless stories of their much-loved Uncle Nino. Not one of them had a bad word to say. They asked me about my mother because they didn't know the story. They'd only been told that their Uncle Nino had fathered a child—a daughter.

Then there were the pictures that Maryann discovered. My pregnant mother, holding hands on the beach with Nino, me sitting on his lap, and many more. Plus the cards . . . all the memorabilia Nino saved. He'd had all of this in his possession until he passed. I wondered how many times he'd looked at everything and wondered about me. Had he ever tried to find me? I'm sure he would have had the means.

I was excited to fly to Florida for the cousins' reunion. Although they were still strangers to me, I had to go. I was so welcomed by every-

one, and they had more photos and family movies to show me! One of the films showed a birthday celebration for the grandma I never got to meet, Autilia. She was sitting at a long table and all the cousins were lined up to kiss her as they walked by. I kept thinking: I should have been in that line. All that great Italian food I missed out on . . . But at least I got my fill of it over the course of our visit. It's great to have an extended family; there's always room for more love.

Six months after my discovery, in August 2018, I joined a Facebook group called NPE Friends. It is a private emotional-support group for those experiencing a Non-Paternal Event or Not-Parent-Expected result. Becoming a member is done through an initial "Gateway" screening where you're asked questions before you get approved. Family members who have been witness to their loved ones' journey are also welcome to join.

I know I've had it a little easier than a lot of my NPE brethren. For one, it was comforting to learn that I was born of a love affair, when many come to learn they're a result of assault, sperm donation, or a one-night stand. The evidence I have today is that I was loved by both Nino and Jack. I also don't have the complexity of additional siblings and/or being accepted or rejected. I just have my thoughts and my story as I have learned it through my family.

I started out in the NPE group needing to be heard and hearing others' stories. Only someone going through something like this could truly understand. I've found comfort and fellowship in this group. When I first joined, there were a little over two thousand members with similar DNA surprises. I soon became a moderator and now help as an administrator for this growing group. Currently, there are now over nine thousand men and women! We've had several retreats and local meet-and-greets that I've helped coordinate in my area. It's been a wonderful support for me.

My DNA journey has had its ups and downs, and I guess I'll always have questions, but it's no longer a heavy burden on my heart. Who I am today is a product of nature and nurture, and I am grateful for all I have. I also accept that it just wasn't God's plan for me to know back then.

Perhaps the most important question I've been asked to reflect on is this: Do I forgive my mother and father?

Forgiveness for me was the intentional decision to let go of the resentment and feelings of betrayal. I can't say I truly ever felt hatred. This doesn't mean I've forgotten, but it frees me from anything that would steal my joy and peace of mind so I can go on with life. When I look back, I can see how the daily stress, bitterness, and constant dwelling on the situation were not beneficial to my life. There was irritability, confusion, anxiousness, and even feelings that were at odds with my spiritual beliefs.

Since my parents were deceased at the time of this discovery, the act of forgiveness fell solely on me. I had to make that commitment and remove the power that feelings of resentment held over me. Because of my close relationship and love for my mother, I could not hold on to any anger towards her. I knew how much she wanted me and loved me. She did some things wrong, but she did so many things right. She had to tuck away a lot of memories and feelings to continue to raise and nurture us, and I'm sure that couldn't have been easy.

I had much more time with my father than my mother since she passed away when I was only thirty-seven years old, but I still had to let go for my own mental well-being. It's too late to physically reconcile with either one of them, and I know that holding onto any resentment is corrosive.

As for Nino, I have no memory of interacting with him, yet he was such a significant figure in my story, too. I had to offer him the same level of forgiveness.

I believe the power of forgiveness flows from God to me and from me to others. In this process, the person who gets healed the most is me. I see so many others in the same situation who say they can never forgive. I hope someday they can see how forgiveness is a release that can bring liberation.

SHARON BETH

During high school, I began to read and appreciate American poetry. In particular, I really liked Emily Dickinson, and one of her poems has become my life's desire, especially now: If I can stop one heart from breaking. This particular poem is so tender and comforting. Maybe it could be of comfort to someone else who is facing pain. —Michelle

Nino and Michelle

EPILOGUE

THE REEL—2024

The film ended and the screen went dark. Suddenly, it hit me! I knew where I'd seen this place before! I logged in to my computer and opened the folder where I'd stored Nino's photos.

I had one picture in my mind. I could see it so clearly . . . I scrolled through the multiple photos, and there it was. In that instant, everything tied together and I finally understood what had been nagging at me while rewatching Grandma Sheila's 8mm beach film.

In Nino's photo, Grandma Sheila is holding my mom's hands and lifting her up in the air. She and my mother are wearing the same swimsuits as in the film. My mother's hair is the same length, combed the same way, and she has the same white barrette in her hair. She is also the same age in the film as she is in the photo. Grandma Sheila's hair is pinned up exactly the same way, and her age is the same, too. The stroller is the same. The background atmosphere is the same.

Unlabeled reel footage from 1955

Then I flipped to the picture of my mother sitting on Nino's lap. In this one, too, she's wearing the same swimsuit and the same white barrette in her hair. And right behind them, in clear sight, is the chain-link fence you can see in Grandma Sheila's film. *Sound View Hotel Guests Only* is written underneath it. There's a low wall, about two to three feet high, between the hotel's forecourt and the beach. You can't get to the beach unless you step down from the wall to the lower ground. This is the step Grandma Sheila takes in the film, as she and my mother make their way toward the water. The building is visible behind them, and the close-up is unmistakably the Sound View Hotel. Everything in Grandma Sheila's 8mm film matches Nino's pictures.

As Nathan said, sometimes the simplest answer *is* the answer. Everything was crystal clear now. How many times had I seen Nino's photographs over the last seven years without making this connection? In that moment, I knew beyond any doubt that

Grandma Sheila's 1955 film was from her and Nino's secret time together at the beach next to the Sound View Hotel, where she'd worked at the Emerald Room. Not only had Nino been present that day, but *he* was the one behind the camera! Not Grandpa Jack! For over two decades, it had been assumed that Grandpa Jack was there on the beach with Grandma Sheila and my mom. That Grandpa Jack was the one behind the camera. Now it was abundantly clear that it wasn't Grandpa Jack, but Nino.

I was right: Grandma Sheila *had* been hiding something! And now I knew why she'd never labeled the film.

I thought back to when we'd viewed the converted films as a family in 2002. It had struck me at the time that Grandpa Jack was silent during this video. As far as I knew, this would have been the first time he'd watched this film. Now I wonder: Could he have been angry? Confused? Maybe he was oblivious? Or just indifferent? We'll never know...

Sound View Hotel postcard, circa, 1912

If I hadn't been writing this book, I might never have revisited this video and made this newer connection. I wouldn't have had any reason to continue studying these films. But I did it because I wanted to watch Grandma Sheila, Grandpa Jack, and my mother together just one more time. I wanted to watch them play and smile and love each other. I didn't expect to unveil more evidence of Grandma Sheila and Nino's love affair.

This single video, together with all the photographs, letters, and knowledge of the affair from family, all finally surfaced and made a full circle back to us. Though their love was silenced, it was not forgotten.

Perhaps Grandma Sheila and Nino wanted their story to be discovered? In addition to the multiple family members who knew about it, Nino kept all the photos and letters for forty-six years until he passed away in 2001, while Grandma Sheila held on to the 8mm film reel for thirty-six years until her death in 1991. They could have thrown it all away, but they didn't. Maybe they wanted my mom to uncover the truth. It's another mystery we'll never solve.

While nearing the end of writing this book, ninety-six-year-old Aunt Jean and I were casually discussing the time period of the affair between Grandma Sheila and Nino, and a couple of details she hadn't shared before surfaced: one of their Rosedale neighbors saw a man—Nino—park his car around the block and walk to Grandma Sheila's house when Grandpa Jack was not home. *Interesting.*

Since we were on the subject, I mustered up the courage to mention once again that the one thing my mom still wished she knew was whether Grandpa Jack knew she wasn't his biological child. After six and a half years of uncertainty following my mom's question, an answer was finally within reach—not a confession to knowing the whole story, but rather the kind of tender, unguarded recall that sometimes comes with age.

"According to the stories I heard, eventually, when my sister Sheila told Jack he wasn't Michelle's father, he made sure that her biological father had nothing to do with her..." said Aunt Jean.

It was confirmed. Grandpa Jack knew.

And it was Grandma Sheila who told him.

There are still many unanswered questions about the details of Grandma Sheila and Nino's relationship, but this happened nearly seventy years ago—sixty-three years, plus the (almost) seven additional years spent trying to figure it out—and I think it's finally time for me to move on.

I've spent more than half my life exploring my family history, and I'm certain there's still more to uncover, but I'm content to hold on to what I have and finally close this chapter.

Until we meet again...

FINAL THOUGHTS

If you are facing your own DNA discovery or any kind of truth-shattering hardship, please know that you are not alone. Healing has no timeline; it's a process, but it can be done. Everyone's suffering is unique, and my mother and I are grateful that our DNA revelation had a positive outcome, knowing that many others do not have the same experience.

Some family members have shared the viewpoint that this DNA discovery was a tragedy and unfair for my mom. We couldn't disagree more. We accept this truth because truth always wins—even if it breaks your heart for a little while. Everyone faces their own challenges, and this was one of ours. Despite the emotional ups and downs that came with this revelation, we recognize that if it weren't for Grandma Sheila and Nino's brief love affair, my mother, sister, and I would not be here today. Our beautiful children also owe their existence to this truth. Therefore, we *are* grateful, accepting, and will continue to cherish our Italian heritage and the tremendous love it has brought us.

We don't know exactly what transpired between Grandpa Jack, Grandma Sheila, and Nino. But I have no doubt that Grandpa Jack loved his daughter, his wife, and his grandchildren.

FINAL THOUGHTS

I can attest to that. Grandpa Jack was a great man, and his legacy will live on through us, regardless of DNA.

Like my mother, I chose to surrender all my pain to God, and, without fail, peace washed over me, just as it had for her. We were no longer drawn into darkness by this revelation. I remember my father once telling me that the only way you can truly be free is to *forgive*. I encourage you to ask God to help you forgive those who hurt you so you can do the same. Let go of the "dead autumn leaves," and be free.

> *. . . But we rejoice in our sufferings knowing that suffering produces endurance, and endurance produces character, and character produces hope, and hope does not put us to shame . . . because God's love has been poured into our hearts through the Holy Spirit . . .*
>
> — ROMANS 5:3-5 HOLY BIBLE, ENGLISH STANDARD VERSION

The End.

ACKNOWLEGEMENTS

Writing and publishing a book has undoubtedly been one of the hardest yet most rewarding experiences! I owe so much gratitude to so many people, but first and foremost, all glory goes to my Heavenly Father. I am nothing without Him.

To Nathan, my amazing husband and best friend—I feel incredibly blessed to share this life with you and for your unconditional love over the past twenty-three years, and I am beyond grateful for your unwavering support throughout this project. Thank you for picking me up when I considered giving up on this book—and there were so many times! You believed in me at every stage and cheered for me as I crossed the finish line. I truly could not have accomplished this book without you by my side. I love you so much.

To my children, you are my sunshine and my constant inspiration in all things. Thank you for teaching me how to be the best version of myself. I'm so blessed to call you mine.

To my dear mother Michelle, I understand that this life-changing event was not an easy journey for you. I am grateful for your love and for entrusting me with this narrative. Thank you

ACKNOWLEGEMENTS

for your bravery and for being a wonderful mother throughout my life. You are remarkable.

To my father Robert, all my gratitude for your love and support throughout my life and this project as well as for sharing your stories with me. You are such a gem.

To my sister Rebecca, thank you for your encouragement throughout this project and for having faith in my ability to tell it. I'm so thankful that we walked this DNA journey together.

To my grandaunt Jean, I will always cherish our weekly Sunday phone calls as you shared countless stories of love with me about our family. It is something I will carry forever, and I can't thank you enough for all your insight. It was such a treasure to celebrate your ninety-sixth birthday together and to read the pages to you in person. I will always love you and value the special bond we share.

To Bonnie, thank you for walking down the genealogy lane with me all these years. Your knowledge has been invaluable and so appreciated! I can't thank you and Mark enough.

To Judy, thank you so much for opening up and speaking with me during those tough times. I really appreciate you.

To Dana, you are like another sister to me. I adore you. I will always treasure the multiple late-night phone calls, texts, and immense love and acceptance you offered my family and me since the beginning of this revelation. I'm so grateful we were reunited as a family.

To Joy, thank you for sharing all the special memories of your mother with me. I hold it all very dear to my heart.

To ALL my family members, both on and off the pages—thank you for your love and support throughout this journey and for opening up to me when I had questions. I am so grateful for all the in-person visits, phone calls, and text chats. May the memories of our lives and the lives of our elders endure. I love you all!

ACKNOWLEGEMENTS

To my *bud*, Ana, it was fun to relive a glimpse of our childhood on these pages—thank you for your support.

I want to express my deepest gratitude to my initial writing coach and editor, Bronwyn Kato, for your incredible vision, unwavering patience, and constant encouragement throughout this journey. You wholeheartedly embraced my story and motivated me to write at my highest potential, allowing us to bring this project to fruition. I genuinely can't thank you enough!

Warmest thanks to my proofreaders, Deirdre Stoelzle and Kelly Messier, for your eagle eyes. You're incredible.

Thank you to Jay Stollman for your willingness to chat and share your memories with a complete stranger. I appreciate it.

Finally, thank you to all my dear friends who supported and cheered for me along the way. It means more than you know.

ABOUT THE AUTHOR

Sharon Beth is a first-time author who resides in Danville, California, with her husband and two teenagers. A 2005 college graduate, she holds two teaching credentials and spent years as a pre-K teacher, fulfilling her passion for education and storytelling. In addition to writing, Sharon enjoys sewing, gardening, and genealogical research. She is a member of the San Ramon Valley Genealogical Society, where she connects with others who share her interest in genealogy. Through her writing, Sharon blends her love of family and life experiences with her desire to inspire and engage her readers.

ABOUT THE AUTHOR

Sharon's book, *Autumn Leaves*, is a deeply personal project that captures her journey throughout the highs and lows of her DNA discovery. She decided to share this struggle in hopes of helping others who carry a similar burden, reassuring them that they are not alone.

RESOURCES

NPE NETWORK

Global support for the Not-Parent-Expected community
   http://www.NPEnetwork.org/
   https://www.facebook.com/NPEnetwork/about

NPE & FRIENDS NETWORK GATEWAY

The private NPE Facebook group that offers private peer-to-peer emotional support group for those who have received unexpected DNA test results.
   https://www.facebook.com/groups/npefriendsgateway

SAN RAMON VALLEY GENEALOGICAL SOCIETY

https://srvgensoc.org/index.php

www.ingramcontent.com/pod-product-compliance
Lightning Source LLC
Chambersburg PA
CBHW020543030426
42337CB00013B/962